What Jesus Meant

GARRY WILLS

What Jesus Meant

VIKING

VIKING
Published by the Penguin Group
Penguin Group (USA) Inc., 375 Hudson Street,
New York, New York 10014, U.S.A.
Penguin Group (Canada), 90 Eglinton Avenue East, Suite 700,
Toronto, Ontario, Canada M4P 2Y3 (a division of Pearson Penguin Canada Inc.)
Penguin Books Ltd, 80 Strand, London WC2R 0RL, England
Penguin Ireland, 25 St. Stephen's Green, Dublin 2, Ireland
(a division of Penguin Books Ltd)
Penguin Books Australia Ltd, 250 Camberwell Road, Camberwell,
Victoria 3124, Australia (a division of Pearson Australia Group Pty Ltd)
Penguin Books India Pvt Ltd, 11 Community Centre,
Panchsheel Park, New Delhi–110 017, India
Penguin Group (NZ), Cnr Airborne and Rosedale Roads, Albany,
Auckland 1310, New Zealand (a division of Pearson New Zealand Ltd)
Penguin Books (South Africa) (Pty) Ltd, 24 Sturdee Avenue,
Rosebank, Johannesburg 2196, South Africa

Penguin Books Ltd, Registered Offices: 80 Strand, London WC2R 0RL, England

First published in 2006 by Viking Penguin, a member of Penguin Group (USA) Inc.

1 3 5 7 9 10 8 6 4 2

ISBN 0-670-03496-7

Printed in the United States of America
Set in Aldus
Designed by Francesca Belanger

TO CELINE
best of sisters

Contents

A Note on Translation

THE MARKETPLACE GREEK of the New Testament—*koinē* ("common denominator") Greek—is not elegant. When Alexander the Great conquered his huge patchwork quilt of different peoples speaking different languages, the only way the defeated could communicate with Macedonian officers, and with other parts of the empire, was in fumbling attempts at the rulers' Greek. When the Romans succeeded the Greek imperial forces, they had to use the language in place, not their own Latin. As Cicero said of the Roman empire, "Greek is read in practically every nation, while Latin is hedged within its own narrow confines" (*Defense of Archias* 23).

In *koinē*, as in any pidgin language, niceties tend to be lost. Words are strung together, often without connectives, to get across a basic meaning. Most of the gospels are written in this basic language, used equally by Romans like Pilate and by Aramaic speakers like Jesus and his followers. Sentences sometimes fumble clumsily at meaning. "What to me and to you, woman?" says Jesus to his mother (Jn 2.4). "Nothing to you and to that just man," says Pilate's wife (Mt 27.19). "The

A NOTE ON TRANSLATION

law and prophets up to John" (Lk 16.16). "I must be at my father's" (Lk 2.49)—his father's what? Commentators quarrel. Definite articles, used according to subtle rules in classical Greek, come and go confusingly in *koinē:* the Lord's Prayer opens with an address to "Our Father in *the* heavens," but a little later in the prayer we get "in heaven and on earth." Tenses shift randomly.

When the meaning is obscure in such a simple language, it is less often because of any sublime meaning conveyed than from mere linguistic clumsiness. Grammar can be muddled, if not neglected altogether. The Book of Revelation is especially ungrammatical—Nietzsche, a trained classicist, said that if God wrote the New Testament, he knew surprisingly little Greek. Except in the Epistle to the Hebrews, the complex sentence structure of classical Greek is rarely evident. We get a simple stringing-on of independent clauses (parataxis) linked repetitively with the boring *kai* ("and"). Dialogue has no elegant variation. It is a matter of "And *X* says . . . And *Y* says . . . And *X* says. . . ."

Most of the words used are common. The infant Jesus is laid in a hay trough *(phatnē)*. But translators know that people expect a "biblical English" in the gospels. They make the hay trough more dignified by using a foreign word (French *manger,* for food) instead of "hay trough." When Jesus answers Pilate, "So you say," they try to find a more elegant form of answer—though "So you say" exactly replicates the

Greek. Translators try to give more churchiness to the evangelists, to teach them their linguistic manners. Jesus should not say to his mother, "What to me and to you, woman?" So they do not let him. Almost every translation into English tries to hide the "faults" of the New Testament. They straighten out the grammar, make the tenses more uniform, break up the repetitions.

If, on the one hand, translators take liberties to spruce up the original, they are slavish in some respects. For instance, instead of translating *Christos,* which means "Anointed," they simply transliterate it. "Anointed" is a title, not a proper name. More important, it is the title of the Messiah. As scholars now emphasize, the word should be translated "Messiah" in Saint Paul's letters, which are the earliest texts in the New Testament, setting many patterns. When Paul says "Christ Jesus," it should be translated "Messiah-Jesus." When he says "Jesus Christ," it is "Jesus-Messiah."

There is a general conservatism in translations, bowing to expectations created by past versions, going back to those with "thees" and "thous" and reverential archaisms. That is why, whenever a new version comes out, it is almost always called undignified. It has departed from the "real" Bible, the King James version. Well, new translations have to be undignified if they are to reproduce the effect of the original. This does not mean that the gospel language lacks force. But it is a rough-hewn majesty, an almost brutal linguistic earthiness. I have tried to capture some of that impact in my translations. They go with the image I have of Jesus himself, a lower-class man speaking the everyday language of his workingmen followers.

The Hebrew scripture is an altogether different matter, on which I have no right to speak. When it is cited here, I use the New English Bible version.

Foreword: Christ Not a Christian

IN CERTAIN RELIGIOUS CIRCLES, the letters WWJD serve as a password or shibboleth. Web sites sell bracelets and T-shirts with the cryptic motto. Some politicians tell us this watchword guides them in making decisions. The letters stand for "What Would Jesus Do?" We are assured that doing the same thing is the goal of real Christians.

But can we really aspire to do what Jesus did? Would we praise a twelve-year-old who slips away from his parents in a big city and lets them leave town without telling them he is staying behind? The reaction of any parent would be that of Jesus' parents: "How could you treat us this way?" (Lk 2.48). Or if relatives seek access to a Christian, should he say that he has no relatives but his followers (Mk 3.33–35)? We might try to change water into wine; but if we did, would we take six huge water vats, used for purification purposes, and fill them with over a hundred gallons of wine, more than any party could drink (Jn 2.6)? If we could cast out devils, would we send them into a herd of pigs, destroying two thousand animals (Mk 5.13)? Some Christians place a very high value on the rights of property, yet this was a massive invasion of some person's property and livelihood.

Other Christians lay great emphasis on family values—should they, like Jesus, forbid a man from attending his own father's funeral (Mt 8.22) or tell others to hate their parents (Mt 8.22, Lk 14.26)? Or should they go into a rich new church in some American suburb, a place taking pride in its success, and whip the persons holding out collection plates, crying, "Make not my Father's house a traders' mart" (Jn 2.16) or "a thieves' lair" (Mk 11.17)? Would it be wise of them to call national religious leaders "whitewashed tombs, pleasant enough to outer appearance, but inside full of dead bones and every rottenness" (Mt 23.27)? Are they justified in telling others, "I come not imposing peace, I impose not peace but the sword" (Mt 10.34)? Or "I am come to throw fire on the earth" (Lk 12.49)? Should they imitate Jesus when he says, "Heaven and earth will pass away, but never will my words pass away" (Mk 21.333)? Or when he says, "I am the resurrection" (Jn 11.25) or "I am the truth" (Jn 14.6), or "I have the authority to lay down my life and I have the authority to take it up again" (Jn 10.18)? None of those who want to imitate Jesus should proclaim that "I am the light of the world" (Jn 8.12) or that "I am the path" to the Father (Jn 14.6).

These are just a few samples of the way Jesus acts in the gospel. They were acts meant to show that he is *not* just like us, that he has higher rights and powers, that he has an authority as arbitrary as God's in the Book of Job. He is a divine mystery walking among men. The only way we can directly imitate him is to act as if we were gods ourselves—yet that is the very thing he forbids. He tells us to act as the last, not the first, as the least, not the greatest. And this accords with the common sense of mankind. Christians cannot really be "Christlike." As Chesterton said, "A great man knows he is not God, and the greater he is the better he knows it." The thing we have to realize is that Christ, whoever or whatever he was, was certainly not a Christian. Romano Guardini put it this way in *The Humanity of Christ*:

If Jesus is a mere man, then he must be measured by the message which he brought to men. He must himself do what he expects of others; he must himself think according to the way he demanded that men think. He must himself be a Christian. Very well, then; the more he is like that, the less he will speak, act, or think as he did; and the more he will be appalled by the blasphemy of the way he did behave. If Jesus is mere man as we are, even though a very profound one, very devout, very pure—no, let us put it another way: the measure of his depth, devotion, purity, reverence, will be the measure in which it will be impossible for him to say what he says. . . . The following clear-cut alternative emerges: either he is—not just evil, for that would not adequately describe the case—either he is deranged, as Nietzsche became in Turin in 1888, or he is quite different, deeply and essentially different, from what we are.

To read the gospels in the spirit with which they were written, it is not enough to ask what Jesus did or said. We must ask what Jesus *meant* by his strange deeds and words. He intended to reveal the Father to us, and to show that he is the only-begotten Son of that Father. What he signified is always more challenging than we expect, more outrageous, more egregious. That is why the Catholic novelist François Mauriac calls him "of all the great characters history places before us, the least logical." Dostoyevsky's Grand Inquisitor knew this when he reproached Christ for puzzling men by being "exceptional, vague, and enigmatic."

It is true that Saint Paul tells us to "put [our] mind in Christ's when dealing with one another" (Phil 2.5). But looking to the mind of Christ is a way of learning what he *meant*, on many levels. We can learn what he valued in the human drama as he moved among his fellows. According to the gospels, he preferred the company of the lowly and despised that of the rich and powerful. He crossed lines of ritual purity to deal with the unclean—with lepers, the possessed, the insane, with prostitutes and adulterers and collaborators with Rome. (Was he subtly mocking ritual purification when he filled the water vessels with wine?) He was called a bastard

(Jn 8.41) and was rejected by his own brothers (Jn 7.3–5) and the rest of his family (Mk 3.21). He was an outcast among outcasts, sharing the lot of the destitute, the defiled, the despised. "He was counted among the outlaws" (Lk 22.37).

He had a lower-class upbringing, as a cabinetmaker's son. That was a trade usually marginal and itinerant in his time. He chose his followers from the lower class, from fishermen, dependent on the season's catch, or from a despised trade (tax collection for the Romans). There were no Scribes or scholars of the Law in his following. Jesus not only favored the homeless. He was himself homeless, born homeless and living homeless during his public life: "Foxes have lairs, and birds have nests in air, but the Son of Man has nowhere to put down his head" (Mt 8.20). He depended on others to shelter him. He especially depended on women, who were "second-class citizens" in his culture. He was not a philosopher. He wrote nothing for his followers in a later age. He depended on his uneducated followers to express what he meant. He knew that the Spirit moving them had no need of men with Ph.D.s or with grants from learned foundations (1 Cor 1.20).

His very presence was subversive. He was born on the run, fleeing Herod. As the Anglican bishop N. T. Wright puts it, he "came into the world with a death sentence already hanging over him, as the paranoid old tyrant up the road got wind of a young royal pretender." Jesus would later move through teams of men setting traps for him, trying to assassinate him, to crush his following, to give him the same treatment given the beheaded John the Baptist. He had to "go into hiding" (Jn 12.36). He was in constant danger—of being kidnapped (Jn 7.30, 7.44), of being arrested (Mt 21.46, Jn 7.32), of being assassinated (Mt 12.14, Lk 13.31, Jn 7.1, 11.53), of being stoned for his irreligion (Jn 8.59, 10.31–33), of being thrown off a cliff (Lk 4.29). Herod Antipas, who killed John the Baptist openly, plotted to kill Jesus secretly (Lk 13.31).

Jesus was called an agent of the devil, or the devil himself (Mk 3.22, Jn 7.20, 8.48, 10.20). He was unclean (Lk 11.38), a consorter with Samaritans (Lk 17.16) and with loose women (Lk 7.39). He was a promoter of immorality (Mk 2.16), a glutton and a drunkard (Lk 7.34), a mocker of the Jewish Law (Mt 12.10, Jn 5.16, 9.16), a schismatic (Jn 8.48). He was never respectable. In fact, he shocked the elders and priests of the Temple when he said, "In truth I tell you, tax collectors and whores are entering God's reign before you" (Mt 21.31). Even when a Pharisee was well disposed to Jesus, he was afraid to be seen with the radical by daylight (Jn 3.1). Jesus seemed to prefer the company of the less-than-respectable, since he said that his Father "favors ingrates and scoundrels" (Lk 6.35). I am reminded of the journalist Murray Kempton, who relished the company of rogues. A political leader once said that Murray would have liked him if only he had a criminal record—though I am sure Murray liked him any-way, from the way he used to tell me good-bye by saying "God bless you," as if we would never meet again.

For two years, Jesus slipped through all the traps set for him. He moved like a fish in the sea of his lower-class fellows. He kept on the move, in the countryside. If I think of a music to be heard in the background of his restless mission, it is the scurrying *agitato* that opens Khachaturian's violin concerto. He went into cities as into alien territory. He was a man of the margins, never quite fitting in, always "out of context." He sought the wilderness, the mountaintop. He gave the slip even to his followers (Mk 7.24). The puzzled disciples trotted behind, trying to make sense of what seemed to them inexplicable, squabbling among themselves about what he was up to. It would never have occurred to them to wear a WWJD bracelet.

Jesus ghosted in and out of people's lives, blessing and cursing, curing and condemning. If he was not God, he was a standing blasphemy against God. The last thing he can be considered is a "gentle Jesus meek and mild." To quote Chesterton again:

We have all heard people say a hundred times over, for they seem never to tire of saying it, that the Jesus of the New Testament is indeed a most merciful and humane lover of humanity, but that the Church has hidden this human character in repellent dogmas and stiffened it with ecclesiastical terrors till it has taken on an inhuman character. This is, I venture to repeat, very nearly the reverse of the truth. The truth is that it is the image of Christ in the churches that is almost entirely mild and merciful. It is the image of Christ in the gospels that is a good many other things as well. The figure in the gospels does indeed utter in words of almost heartbreaking beauty his pity for our broken hearts. But they are very far from being the only sort of words that he utters. . . . There is something appalling, something that makes the blood run cold, in the idea of having a statue of Christ in wrath. There is something insupportable even to the imagination in the idea of turning the corner of a street or coming out into the spaces of a marketplace, to meet the petrifying petrifaction of that figure as it turned upon a generation of vipers, or that face as it looked at the face of a hypocrite. . . . [The gospel story] is full of sudden gestures evidently significant except that we hardly know what they signify; of enigmatic silences; of ironical replies. The outbreaks of wrath, like storms above our atmosphere, do not seem to break out exactly where we should expect them, but to follow some higher weather chart of their own. The Peter whom popular Church teaching presents is very rightly the Peter to whom Christ said in forgiveness, "Feed my lambs." He is not the Peter upon whom Christ turned as if he were the devil, crying in that obscure wrath, "Get thee behind me, Satan." Christ lamented with nothing but love and pity over Jerusalem which was to murder him. We do not know what strange spiritual atmosphere or spiritual insight led him to sink Bethsaida lower in the pit than Sodom.

The Jesus of the gospels is scandalous, and one of those scandalized was Thomas Jefferson. He was so offended by the miracles and the curses, by the devils assailing and defeated, that he created his own more acceptable Jesus, excising all those parts of the gospels that he considered unworthy of a wise man's story. The result, cleansed of all the supernatural hocus-pocus, is the tale of a good man, a very good man, perhaps the best of good men—therefore a man who would not pretend to work miracles, to wrestle with demons, or to have unique access to God the Father. Jefferson's revised New Testament is not only much shorter than the real one but much duller. Nothing unexpected occurs in it. There is, for instance, no Resurrection. Jefferson's Jesus is shorn of his paradoxes and left with platitudes. He is a man of his time, or even ahead of his time, but not outside time, whereas the Jesus of the gospels is both temporal and above time. As Chesterton concludes:

There is more of the wisdom that is one with surprise in any simple person, full of the sensitiveness of simplicity, who should expect the grass to wither and the birds to drop dead out of the air, when a strolling carpenter's apprentice said calmly and almost carelessly, like one looking over his shoulder: "Before Abraham was, I am."

Needless to say, that verse (Jn 8.58) is excised by Jefferson. His mild humanitarian moralizer is not allowed to say anything shocking, challenging, or obscure. Devils and miracles are not the only things to go. So are passages like this:

"Think not I come imposing peace to earth. I come bringing not peace but a sword. I bring conflict between a man and his father, a daughter and her mother, a wife and her mother-in-law—a man's foes will be found in his own home. One who loves father or mother before me does not deserve me. One who loves son or daughter before me does not deserve me. And anyone who does not take up a cross and tread in my footsteps does not deserve me. The man protective of his life will lose it, but the one casting life away on my account will preserve it." (Mt 10.34–39)

Jefferson's extraction of the "real" gospel from the traditional one—a task he called as easy as "finding diamonds in dunghills"—has been taken up in recent years by a team that finds the task more difficult, but productive of much the same result. This team of scholars calls itself the Jesus Seminar, and it prints a Bible that sets apart by different colors the "authentic" sayings or deeds of Jesus and the sayings invented by the evangelists or their sources. Though these experts use linguistic and historical tests for qualifying the diamonds in their dunghill, they work from a Jeffersonian assumption that anything odd or dangerous or supernatural is prima facie suspect. That disqualifies the Resurrection from the outset. The Seminar's founder, Robert Funk, agreed with Jefferson that Jesus was "a secular sage," and the team trims the gospels even more thoroughly than Jefferson did. One whole gospel, John, has no authentic saying (Jefferson liked quite a lot of John). Most of Mark (usually counted the most authentic gospel, since it is the earliest) also falls by the wayside, along with the last three and a half chapters of Matthew. Luke, as the most "humanist gospel," comes off best, but overall the Seminar retains fewer than a fifth of the gospel acts of Jesus and fewer than a fifth of his words.

This is the new fundamentalism. It believes in the literal sense of the Bible—it just reduces the Bible to what it can take as literal quotation from Jesus. Though some people have called the Jesus Seminarists radical, they are actually very conservative. They tame the real radical, Jesus, cutting him down to their own size. Robert Funk called Jesus "the first Jewish stand-up comic"—which is not as far as it might at first glance seem from Jefferson's view of him as the last sit-down Stoic sage.

Of course, the sayings that meet with the Seminar's approval were preserved by the Christian communities whose contribution is discounted. Jesus as a person does not exist outside the gospels, and the only reason he exists there is because of their authors' faith in the Resurrection. Trying to find a construct, "the historical Jesus," is not like finding diamonds in a dunghill, but like finding New York City at the bottom of the Pacific Ocean. It is a mixing of categories, or rather of wholly different worlds of discourse. The only Jesus we have is the Jesus of faith. If you reject the faith, there is no reason to trust anything the gospels say. The Jesus of the gospels is the Jesus preached, who is the Jesus resurrected. Belief in his continuing activity in the members of his mystical body is the basis of Christian belief in the gospels. If that is unbelievable to anyone, then why should that person bother with him? The flat cutout figure they are left with is not a more profound philosopher than Plato, a better storyteller than Mark Twain, or a more bitingly ascetical figure than Epictetus (the only ancient philosopher Jefferson admired). If his claims are no higher than theirs, then those claims amount to nothing.

With certain religious figures, the original story that reaches us does not begin with literal facts that are later "embellished," as the Seminarists put it. The first reports spreading from such figures are all a blaze of holiness and miracle. That is as true of Saint Francis as of the Baal Shem Tov. It is their impact on the faith of others that makes these men noticeable in the first place. Miracles, as it were, *work themselves* around such men. Jesus is the preeminent example of this. The fact that he seems like other wonder-working holy men—Apollonius of Tyana, for instance—does not mean that he is an imitation of them. Rather, they are a reaching out toward him. They are a hunger and he the food. They are an ache, he the easement. As Chesterton said, his story resembles the great myths of mankind because he is the fulfillment of the myths. When someone said that other stories tell of God's voice coming from heaven, and so does the scene of Christ's baptism, therefore his story must be just like the other ones, Chesterton asked, "From what place could a voice of God come, from the coal cellar?"

In the case of Jesus, the first blaze of wonder and miracle is registered in the letters of Paul, which preceded the gospels by a quarter to half of a century. The Seminarists treat the gospels as if they were just a distortion of the "real" sayings of Jesus that preceded them. But what preceded them in fact was the testimony of Paul, who already preached the divinity of Christ, his descent from the Father, his saving death and Resurrection. Nor can we say that he invented something different from the gospels, as if they were already in existence. He is passing on what was given to him in the

Christian community (1 Cor 15.3). We know this is the case because he quotes hymns of the community that preceded his letters, including this one:

> He, having the divine nature from the outset,
>   thinking it no usurpation to be held God's equal,
> emptied himself out into the nature of a slave,
>   becoming like to man.
> And in man's shape he lowered himself,
>   so obedient as to die, by a death on the cross.
> For this God has exalted him,
>   favored his name over all names,
> that at the name of Jesus all knees shall bend
>   above the earth, upon the earth, and below the earth,
> and every tongue shall acknowledge
>   that Jesus is the Lord Christ, to the glory of God the
>   Father.   (Phil 2.6–11)

The proclamation of divinity is not something "added on" later. It is the very thing to which all later explanations are added. The gospels, following on this profession of an active and shared faith, trace the theological implications of that faith, and cite Jesus' words only in the context of that belief, the only context that exists for them. So this book will accept what Jesus meant as conveyed to us by what the gospels mean. It will treat the Jesus of faith, since there is no other. The "historical Jesus" does not exist for us. Romano Guardini put the matter well in his book on the psychology of Jesus:

> Were we in a position to disregard all [later] accounts and gain an immediate impression of Jesus Christ as he was on earth, we would not be confronted by a "simple" historical Jesus, but by a figure of devastating greatness and incomprehensibility. Progress in the representation of the portrait of Christ does not mean that something was being added to what was proclaimed; it means that we are witnessing the unfolding step by step of that which "was from the beginning." . . . If we could get back to the "original," that is, if we could work our way back to the picture of Christ as it existed before it had been turned over in the apostles' minds or elaborated by their preaching, before it had been assimilated by the corporate life of the faithful, we could find a figure of Christ even more colossal and incomprehensible than any conveyed by even the most daring statements of St. Paul or St. John. . . . The statements of the apostles are guides to him which never quite do justice to the fullness of his divine-human natures. The apostles never state more about the historical Jesus than he actually was; it is always less.

To accept the gospels as an authentic account of what Jesus meant should not make us revert from the new fundamentalism to the old one, treating everything in the gospels as literally true in a later sense of historical truth. The gospels express the ineffable in the language appropriate for the task, a language inherited from the Jewish scriptures. Luke's gospel, for instance, spells out the meaning of Christ's Incarnation in the poetic forms of divine birth, because he and his fellows knew that this is what the Christ event *meant*. To believe in the gospels is to take everything in them as meant, though at various levels of symbolization. To read the gospels reverently is to keep asking, through all such symbols, what Jesus means. That is my purpose here.

This is not a scholarly book but a devotional one. It is a profession of faith—a reasoning faith, I hope, and reasonable; what Saint Anselm called "faith out on quest to know" (*fides quaerens intellectum*). In writing it, I had in mind certain devotional treatments of Jesus written by fellow Catholics—especially those by Gilbert Chesterton (*The Everlasting Man*), François Mauriac (*Life of Jesus*), Romano Guardini (*The Human Christ*), and Shusaku Endo (*A Life of Jesus*). These men were not scripture scholars, just firm believers who read the gospels carefully, with the insights their own faith gave them. Endo consciously imitated Mauriac, and I have tried to follow the lead of both men; but each of the writers mentioned, in his own way, helped me see the radicalism of the gospels. Mauriac also brought home to me this humbling truth:

No doubt a life of Jesus should be written on one's knees, with a feeling of unworthiness great enough to make the pen drop from the hand. A sinner should blush for his temerity in undertaking such a work.

Or, as a greater guide avowed, "I am not up to the task of touching his sandal" (Mt 3.11).

1. The Hidden Years

His Birth Announced

FOR ME, the most convincing pictures or sculptures of the Annunciation to Mary show her in a state of panic. Arturo Martini and Dante Gabriel Rossetti show her shrinking off from the angel, looking cornered by him. Lorenzo Lotto shows her turning entirely away from the angel, as if about to run from him. But the most striking images occur in fourteenth-century paintings—by, for instance, Lorenzo Veneziano and the Master of the Cini Madonna—where Mary is made so faint by the angel's words that she sways back and must grab a pillar to keep herself upright.

This reaction is signaled by the gospel of Luke, which says, "She was deeply shaken [*dietarachthē*] by what the angel said, and was trying to puzzle out [*dielogizeto*] what such a greeting could mean" (Lk 1.29). The angel has to reassure her: "Have no fear, Mary, this is because you have found favor with God." Did she know already how dangerous is such favor? God's chosen people are commonly chosen to suffer. Of Jesus in particular, John Henry Newman wrote: "All who came near him more or less suffered by approaching him,

1

just as if pain and trouble went out of him, as some precious virtue for the good of their souls." Jesus says as much in his ironic description of a Christian happiness: "Happy are you when others revile you, afflict you, bring filthy false charges against you for following me. Take comfort and be glad, since great will be your recompense in heaven. That is how they afflicted the prophets before you" (Mt 5.11–12).

Mary will soon be told what to expect from her divine privilege. When she presents her newborn child in the Temple, she is told by the saintly Jewish elder Simeon, "This very child is marked to be a sign of contradiction, for the downfall or uplifting of many in Israel, while a sword will run through this woman's heart, to lay bare the inner divisions of many a mind" (Lk 2.34–35).

The child himself will say, in his maturity, "Think not I come to impose peace on the earth, I come imposing not peace but a sword" (Mt 10.34). Later generations will justify crusades from such words, but the sword Jesus bears will be used against him and his, not by them. To Peter he says, "Put your sword back in its holder—those taking up the sword die of the sword" (Mt 26.52). The sword he brings is wielded by others—in the first (and immediate) case by the Jewish collaborator with Rome, Herod, who kills children indiscriminately while trying to find the dangerous baby who has quietly infiltrated his realm. From the outset, Jesus is a threat to power.

He begins as a mysterious rumor, one child hidden among the many, who are put at risk by his radical presence among them. He is extraordinary, but at the same time he is indistinguishable from other babies. The angel gives him his name, not leaving that to the discretion of either parent—yet the name Jesus was one of the most common of his time, as the first-century Jewish historian Josephus tells us. It is as if he were called Everyman—or simply the Son of Man. He seems at first the exemplar, or a summary, of all mankind, though that impression will be proved false, since the simple name of Jesus will, as the early Christian hymn says, be favored "over all names, that at the name of Jesus all knees shall bend above the earth, upon the earth, and below the earth, and every tongue shall acknowledge that Jesus is the Lord Christ, to the glory of God the Father" (Phil 2.9–11).

Displaced Person

JESUS IS MULTIPLY DISPLACED, made peripheral to the important places of the world. He comes from a despised city and region (Jn 1.46). Yet he cannot be allowed a peaceful birth in that backwater. His parents are displaced by decree of an occupying power that rules his people. For the imperial census to be taken, Joseph his father must return to his place of birth. The Jews feared and resented authority when it took to counting them for the better control of their lives. This was true even when their own ruler, David, took a census (2 Sam 24.1–25). Luke indicates that Rome's power is tyrannical when his gospel shows the emperor shuffling the lives of distant people.

Joseph does not even have relatives left in his native town, people with whom he can stay. He seeks shelter in an inn, already crowded with people taken away from their own homes and lives. Because of this influx of strangers, he is turned away. There is no bed left, even for a woman far advanced in pregnancy. She must deliver her child in a barn, where the child is laid in a hay trough *(phatnē)*. The extrusion from normal surroundings and circumstances is complete. Not only is he born into an oppressed people, and forced out of his parent's city, and excluded from the common shelter—now the oppressed person, the homeless person, the excluded person must become a fugitive, driven farther away from the familiar, the comfortable, into an exile that recalls the wandering of the whole Jewish people. Herod the persecutor takes up the role formerly played by Pharaoh, the men of power trying to stamp out God's chosen instrument—first his People, then his Son. The relationship of Jesus to worldly power is revealed from the very outset of his life. He is the rulers' prey, on the run from them down through the ages.

Young Manhood

IN THE EARLIEST GOSPEL, that of Mark, Jesus appears out of nowhere, a mature man, to announce that God's reign has arrived. Luke (3.23) says that Jesus was "about thirty" at the time—but that is just the conventional way of saying that he was fully adult. What was Jesus doing in the preceding time, in what have been called his "hidden years"? Luke says that he "grew physically and mentally" (2.52), after giving us a scene that symbolizes this process. The progressive detachment from his family that all adolescents undergo is described at the onset of Jesus' adolescence, the age of twelve, when Jesus leaves his parents without informing them that he is doing so. This occurs in Jerusalem, where his parents have brought him to observe the holy days. He slips away from them in order to "sit with the scholars in the Temple, hearing them and asking them questions" (3.46). He must learn about the revelations to his people.

His unexplained disappearance naturally disconcerts his parents, who have traveled homeward a whole day without realizing that he has left their party. After three frantic days of searching for him, they find him in the Temple, and Mary asks, "How could you do this to us? Can you not see how disturbed your father and I were while we looked for you?" Jesus in effect declares his independence of worldly father and mother by answering, "Why would you look for me?

Could you not tell that I must be at my Father's?" (Lk 2.49). But "they did not understand what he was saying" (2.50). He was a mystery in his own home. Other members of his family will be at a similar loss in coping with this disturbing person in their midst. When his public life becomes controversial, "not even his brothers gave him credence" (Jn 7.5). Indeed, "his family tried to take him into custody" (Mk 3.21). After making a stir elsewhere, he tried to return to Nazareth, his native village, but the inhabitants "ganged up to throw him out of town, taking him to the edge of the cliff on which the town was built, with the intention of throwing him over" (Lk 4.29).

The independence Jesus had shown in leaving his parents to haunt the Temple was obviously shown to other members of his family, to the brothers and sisters mentioned in Mt 13.55, to "his brothers James, Joseph, Judas, and Simon" (Mk 6.3). The frequently emphasized hostility he experienced from his own family helps us understand the shocking ease with which Jesus could later say, "If one coming to me does not hate his father and his mother, and his wife and children, and his brothers and sisters—and, for that matter, his own life—he cannot be my follower" (Lk 14.26). For members of his own family, such an attitude was itself hateful. They could not see why he put on airs, went a different way, learned things beyond them, spent time on Hebrew texts that only scholars could deal with, neglecting (no doubt) the family business of cabinetmaking.

Jesus would later praise Mary, the sister who leaves do-
mestic chores to listen to him, over Martha, who does the
necessary housework while he is visiting them (Lk 10.38–41).
Do we get a glimpse here of his own attitude toward the
humdrum lives of the people he grew up with? He had a
more urgent mission, the affairs of his Father, than the
games and tasks of other children. Though we are not explic-
itly told anything about "the hidden years" beyond Luke's
description of his running away from his parents when he
was twelve, the stance of the rebel who would not be contained in the expectations of his hometown comes out again
and again when family ties are mentioned. At a wedding in
Cana, where some of his old townspeople from Nazareth are
present, he says to his mother, "What to me and to you,
woman?" (Jn 2.4). When a woman says that the womb bearing him was a blessed one, he answers, "Blessed, rather, those
who, hearing God's word, are its champions" (Lk 11.27–28).
When he is told that his mother and brothers are seeking access to him, he says, "Who is my mother, who my brothers?"
Then, looking around the circle of his followers, he adds,
"Here, you see, is my mother, here my brothers. The person
who does what God wills, that person is my brother, my sister, my mother" (Mk 3.33–35).

Christian leaders have often rebuked the rebelliousness of
young people by offering them a pastel picture of the young
Jesus as a model of compliance and good behavior. They
make this mystifying child an exemplar of "family values"

in the most restricting and conformist sense. But there are many indications that Jesus was more like those restive and resisting children who have all the idealism and absolutism of youth—young people who chafe against the boundaries of the past and are panting to explore new horizons. We are told that his brothers and sisters later considered him "mad" (Mk 3.21). It was a view they had probably formed from their earliest experiences with him.

When an exceptional child defies expectations, it is a loving mother who is often most puzzled and concerned by the family tensions this causes. Some of this parental quandary is well presented in Mary Gordon's novel *Pearl,* where a mother is forced to question her own identity when her child takes a radical stand on principle that might end her life. The mother of Jesus felt such puzzlement and concern to a greater degree, given the depth of the mystery she had brought forth from her own body. She is "deeply shaken" by the angel's indication of her child's destiny and "tries to puzzle out" its meaning (Lk 1.29). When Simeon added to the mystery, during Jesus' presentation in the Temple, she was "astounded at what was being said" (Lk 2.33). When the twelve-year-old in the Temple tells her and Joseph that they should not have looked for him, "they did not understand what he was saying" (Lk 2.50), though Mary kept trying to understand: "She kept these things for inner scrutiny, sifting them in her heart" (Lk 2.19). No doubt she went through the same pained questioning when Jesus refused to receive her (Mk 3.32).

Jesus' Vocation

LUKE SAYS THAT after Jesus was found in the Temple by his parents, he returned with them to their home in Nazareth, "and obeyed them" (Lk 2.51), but he does not say how long he stayed there. If he was "about thirty" when he came before the public, that covers not only his adolescence but his young manhood, the period of (roughly) his twenties. Did Jesus marry in this time? That would have been normal for a young Jewish man, and especially for an observant one. That is why biblical scholars assume that Paul was married in his days as a Pharisee, though he is single again by the time he writes his epistles. His wife could have died, or left him, or been put aside under Jewish law.

But Jesus was not educated as a Pharisee, like Paul. He enters his adult ministry from the radical ascetic movement that was critical of the Jewish establishment. He came from the remote retreats of men like the Essenes and the Baptist—that "voice crying from the desert" (Mk 1.3)—where celibacy was a prized discipline. The various groups of Essenes, including one strain in the Qumran community (librarians of the Dead Sea Scrolls), were dissidents from the cult of the Second Temple (that built by the Romans' tool, Herod). They believed in a restoration of the true Israel, relying on the prophets who excoriated an Israel gone astray. They were a people set apart even from the nation that was set apart by God, caught up more in eschatological drama than in the settled ways of Temple observance. Jesus and his disciples will turn, too, to the prophets, and predict the fall of Herod's Temple.

It was probably among such desert ascetics and scholars, rather than in Pharisaical classes, that Jesus learned Hebrew. This was the learned language of his day. What common folk spoke was the indigenous Aramaic. Their necessary second language in everyday life was "marketplace Greek," the language of the empire that Rome inherited from Alexander's Greek successors. It was the inability of ordinary Jews to understand Hebrew that made it necessary to translate all their scripture into Greek. Jesus would have spoken Greek to Pontius Pilate, since Pilate did not know Aramaic and Jesus did not know Latin. None of the first disciples understood Latin. Jesus did not learn Hebrew in his home. Lower-class people like his parents did not commonly know Hebrew. In fact his parents, like almost all the lower class in Palestine (or, for that matter, like most poor people in antiquity), were very likely illiterate. To learn Hebrew and study the Bible texts he had to go out to those mystics. It was natural, therefore, for his first recorded association to be with John the Baptist. Repeatedly in the gospels he surprises those around him by his learning, which would show first in his knowledge of Hebrew (Mt 13.54, Mk 1.22, Lk 2.47, Jn 7.15). This was not a knowledge his fishermen followers possessed—though his first mentors in the desert would have had it, and passed it on to him.

All four gospels place the beginning of Jesus' ministry in the context of John the Baptist's radical reform movement. He allies himself with a wild man, raggedly clad in animal skins, who denounces those coming near him as "vipers' offspring" (Lk 3.7). If the young Jesus went off into the desert, giving up the hopes of his family for any offspring to support them, this rejection of family is what caused their later hostility to him. He was making a radical break with life, as most people envisaged and praised it, to become a spiritual "extremist." When he moved from the spiritual isolation of the Essenes to the activist denunciations of the Baptist, that would have dismayed his family even more profoundly. They would have felt what families feel today when their sons or daughters join a "cult."

The gospels of Matthew and Luke (the latter is most interested in Jesus' education) spell out the meaning of his desert experience. They describe the "trying" (*peirasmos*, Lk 4.13) of Jesus after his induction into John's discipline of baptism, but their method makes it clear that they are summing up a whole process—the spiritual quest during his adolescence and young manhood—under the symbol of one event, the encounter with Satan in the desert. In presenting Jesus with three challenges, the gospels present the competing "career tracks" he was being asked to consider—only to see that Jesus rejects them all. Jesus is arriving, by an intense inner scrutiny and self-experiment, at his true vocation. His own *peirasmos* reflects the world-wrenching that the Essenes contemplated and anticipated in their apocalyptic theology. Jesus himself will later describe the *Peirasmos* that will end time in a terrifying final judgment. His followers must pray to escape the fires of that *Peirasmos* (Mt 6.13, Lk 22.46).

By undergoing his personal trial, he bears things he would protect others from—as he does in his later testing in the garden of Gethsemane. He is already in that sense rescuing them as he faces his solitary ordeal. The testing in the desert is not only a symbol of his own growth into a knowledge of his calling. It is a symbolic presentation, here at the beginning of his public life, of his whole salvific function, taking up the burden of all mankind. The three tests in the desert present in synecdoche (part for whole) the drama behind the outer events of his ministry.

The subtlety of the tests is what makes them insidious. Each is an apparently slight—but fatal—distortion of the real mission of Jesus. If Satan can get Jesus to accept this diminished version of his calling, the Prince of this World will retain his hold upon history. Everything will depend on Jesus' getting the Father's will just right.

The First Test

"THEN THE DEVIL TOLD HIM: 'If you are in fact God's Son, tell this stone to become bread.' " Bread for the poor is one way of looking at the reign of heaven that Jesus brings to mankind:

Mary's proclamation on the destiny of her son (the Magnificat) contains these words: "He has filled abundantly whoever hungers, and sent the rich off destitute" (Lk 1.53).

All four gospels show Jesus miraculously feeding bread to vast numbers of people (Mt 14.21, Mk 6.44, 8.8, Lk 9.14, Jn 6.10).

Jesus tells his followers to feed the poor, saying that a failure to do that is a way of starving him (Mt 25.42–45).

If all these things are true, then why does Jesus reject the devil's invitation to turn lifeless stone to life-giving bread? Some will claim that they are serving Jesus by doing just that. The political left thinks in terms of Christian socialism. The political right thinks in terms of a providential Invisible Hand (the marketplace) that feeds the poor. But Jesus does not come to bring mankind a higher politics. A religion that limits itself to assuaging earthly hunger seals off the greater promise of God's reign, his justice *(dikaiosynē)* that is a judgment. He says, instead, "Happy those hungering and thirsting for God's Judgment—they will be satisfied" (Mt. 5.6).

Jesus is not a social reformer. John the Baptist was a reformer in the mold of the ancient prophets. John tells religious leaders not to be proud, and tax collectors to avoid graft, and soldiers not to agitate for more pay (Lk 3.7–14). He warns of a coming judgment, but his work is all preparatory, his baptism is simply an intensification of the ritual cleansings of the Law. Jesus will baptize with fire, not water (Lk 3.16). It is a fire from heaven, opening a whole new level of life.

Marx said that religion drugs man with heavenly hopes that take away the need to do good here and now. There is another way that religion can become an opiate—by satisfying earthly needs, making heavenly aspirations unnecessary, occluding broader horizons. Jesus will not be satisfied with anything that holds the Father to a lesser glory than he promises.

In reply to the first test, then: "Jesus answered him: 'Scripture tells us, bread alone does not give man his life' " (Lk 4.4).

The Second Test

SATAN RATCHETS UP his probing. If Jesus wants greatness of spirit as well as physical satiation, what exultation of the spirit does the world promise?

"Lifting him up, then, he showed him, in a single glance, every realm in the world. And the devil said: 'All their power and all their glory I will bestow on you, since they are entrusted to me and to those I bestow them on. Bow to me and it is all yours' " (Lk 4.5–7).

It is not temporal power alone that Satan offers. When he says the realms will come with "all their glory," he is including rule over the spirit of mankind. In effect, he is offering Jesus what will become the medieval papacy, with its all-encompassing authority over "the two swords" of temporal rule and spiritual rule. It is generally agreed now that the church should not rule the state; but of the two powers exercised in the Middle Ages, the more insidious threat, offering the most intense corruption, was spiritual rule. This led popes to kill souls by interdicts (forbidding all access to the sacraments in realms they wanted to control) and to pretensions that as pope they could exempt people from Purgatory for payments rendered. This truly was to make the Father's house a traders' mart (Jn 2.16) and a thieves' lair (Mk 11.17). Those popes forgot that Jesus was harshest on his first followers when they aspired to authority over others, to be first when they should be last, to put on the airs of the Pharisees:

> "Do not be called Rabbi, since you have only one teacher, and you are all brothers. And call no one on earth your father, since you have only one Father, the one in heaven. And do not be called leaders, since you have only one leader, the Messiah. Rather, let the greatest among you be servant to the others. For whoever lifts himself up will be abased, and whoever abases himself will be lifted up." (Mt 23.8–12)

In reply to the second test, then: "Jesus answered him: 'Scripture tells us, to the Lord alone will you bow, and him only serve'" (Lk 4.8).

The Third Test

MATTHEW MAKES THE OFFER of all earthly realms the cul-
minating test, giving as the second test what Luke makes
the climactic one. Luke's account is more finely nuanced.
Matthew thinks of rule as the supreme offer. Luke knows
better. He, like the devil, sees that Jesus' very sense of a divine calling is also his most dangerous claim:

> Then he took him to Jerusalem, and placed him on
> the Temple's pinnacle, and said: "If you are God's Son,
> throw yourself down from here, since scripture tells us:
> He will order his angels to keep you in their care. It
> says: They will hold you up in their hands, so you harm
> not your foot on the rocks." (Lk 4.9–11)

Satan knows that the real challenge to his power in the
universe is not any earthly rule that Jesus could aspire to,
but his sense of his own special relationship to the Father. If
he can get Jesus to presume on that, or separate it from sub-
missiveness to the Father, he defeats the Father, making Jesus
repeat the presumption of Eve when she thought she could
become godlike in her own right. Satan will top the fall of
man with the fall of Man. The Jesus of John's gospel recognizes this danger, and obviates it. His own divinity is a divinity in the Father, not apart from him. He will not test the

Father, because he is too closely identified with him. It would be putting himself on trial. As he says in John's gospel: "The Son, I tell you in truth, can do nothing but what he sees the Father doing. And whatever he does, the Son does in his turn. For the Father loves the Son, and shows him whatever he does" (Jn 5.19–20).

In reply to the third test, then: "Jesus answered him: 'Scripture tells us: You will not experiment upon the Lord, your God' " (Lk 4.12–13).

What Jesus rejects, in arriving at his real vocation, is any notion of a "cheap salvation." Dostoyevsky, in his famous meditation on this episode, has Spain's Grand Inquisitor rebuke Jesus for not accepting a cheap salvation as a way of sparing his followers from the heroic loneliness that Jesus is capable of but they are not. He should feed them bread and miracles and authority, as a way of making life bearable amid so many pains and disheartening burdens. But Jesus does not want to make life bearable, as a way of easing the path through time. He wants to make his followers leap outside of time, to see things in the stark reality of the Father's judgment on those who blunt spiritual capacity with melioratives.

What the temptation in the desert dramatizes is Jesus' deepening realization of what the Father asks of him, and what in his name he must ask of others. Great men often have such a young period of anguish over the vocation dimly making itself clear, to their fascination and revulsion. The historian Arnold Toynbee generalized this pattern as "withdrawal and return" in the formation of great men. The more relevant consideration for Jesus is the parallel with the Jewish people's trial in the wilderness—forty years of advance toward the chosen land—that is formalized by Luke under the rubric of forty days for Jesus' ordeal. At the end of this most important process of spiritual formation, in which he knew hunger and denial, he is strengthened and comforted, angels bringing him food (Mt 4.11), just as the people of Israel were fed with manna in the desert. Jesus is now spiritually tempered and toughened for his great work. The testing and formative time is over, the desert ordeal ended. That is the meaning of the hidden years.

2. The Work Begins

The Baptist

JESUS COMES BEFORE THE WORLD as a follower of John the Baptist. His own mission is permanently interwoven with John's, a fact symbolized in their parallel birth narratives and their paired deaths by Roman execution. They are cousins, born almost at the same time (John is six months older). Yet John will acknowledge that "Greater than I is the one who comes after me" (Mk 1.7). When John protests that he is not worthy to baptize Jesus, the latter assures him: "Let be for now, so we may observe all that is laid out for us" (Mt 3.15). As usual, a process is dramatized as an event—the gradual emergence of Jesus from the tutelage of John. John is a halfway station between the asceticism of the desert and the radical freedom of Jesus' full ministry. John recognizes the greater destiny toward which his pupil is moving, and—unlike many teachers—he does not check this growth but promotes it.

Admittedly, Jesus' later course will puzzle John. Not only does Jesus move away from his ascetical beginnings. Very soon he is mixing easily, too easily, it is said, with very worldly people. It is not simply that he does not fast, like John. He does not even keep the eating code of the orthodox. He eats with the unclean, with prostitutes, with Roman collaborators. It seemed to some that he was betraying the mission of John, who had been a scourge of lax ways, a man who lived in a perpetual heroism of penitence. The murmurings began early and would intensify as Jesus took a course very different from John's in the desert, as well as from that of priests in the cities: "So they said to him: 'The followers of John fast continually and pray. So for that matter do the Pharisees. But your followers are eaters and drinkers.' But he answered: 'Can you force a bridegroom's party to fast in his presence at the wedding? The time will come when the groom is gone, and that will be the time for fasting' " (Lk 5.33–35). Jesus knew all the talk about him, and summed it up himself: "The Son of Man has arrived eating and drinking and you say: 'This man is a glutton and drunkard, the associate of tax collectors and the unclean' " (Lk 7.34). For Jesus to be called a glutton and a drunkard was not a light criticism. It was based on a matter of Levitical law. In Deuteronomy 21.20, that is the description of a son rebelling against the people's way, the basis of a charge before the elders of the tribe that leads to death by stoning. Jesus is so radical that he needs execution.

Eventually reports about Jesus unsettled John himself. What was he up to? Was he still capable of the messianic hopes John had placed in him? He sent two of his own followers to sound Jesus out. "When these men reached Jesus, they told him: 'John the Baptist has sent us to ask you: Are you the one we hope for, or should we look to another?' " Jesus answered by citing the messianic signs of the prophets: "Return to John and report what you see and hear—blind men see, lame men walk, lepers are cleansed, deaf men hear, and poor men hear the revelation of God. Happy the man who finds no obstacle in me" (Lk 7.22–23).

When John's messengers are gone, Jesus spells out his relationship with John. "What did you expect to find in the desert—a reed flexible in the wind? What did you go there to see—one clothed in fine raiment? No, it is in palaces that you find men reveling in fine raiment and soft living. What, then, did you go to see? A prophet? Indeed. And I tell you something further, that he is more than a prophet. He is the one scripture foretold: 'I send my emissary out before you, to mark out the path for your coming.' I tell you no man born of woman is greater than John—though the least person in God's reign is greater than he" (Lk 7.24–28).

God's reign. That is what Jesus has brought to humankind. That is the wedding party at which he is the bridegroom, the party he is celebrating with his ragged crew of outcasts. What is God's reign?

Calling Others

JESUS, in the process of detaching himself from John's other followers, began to form his own circle around him. He calls men not from the desert but from the working class. The first disciples are not ascetics but fishermen, unlearned men, married men. They are drawn to his evident holiness. He is charismatic in the original and full sense, a man graced, set apart by God. What was the source of this charm?

We do not know what Jesus looked like. Presumably, since he was a Jewish man, he looked like a Jewish man. But that does not get us far, since there is no one type (or stereotype) of a Jewish man. Some imagine that only a perfect human physique could be worthy of housing the incarnate Word of God. But that, too, is not very helpful, since ideals of human perfection vary. Was he a perfect athlete, muscular and graceful, or a more sensitive and poetic man? Some think he had to have every masculine quality carried to its height of perfection. Others feel that he could only express the fullness of humanity by combining the strong points of both genders.

My own guess is that any attempt to Christianize the Apollo Belvedere and call him Jesus takes us down the wrong path. The holy person is often slight and frail, with spiritual powers fretting their physical envelope. That was the case with many saints, whether Saint Francis or the Baal Shem Tov or the Quaker Anthony Benezet. People instinctively feel the companionship of such men with the afflicted. The energy radiating from them has partly consumed them. They burn with banked fires and they are in the fires. In the words of Chesterton: "St. Francis was a lean and lively little man, thin as a thread and vibrant as a bowstring. In appearance he must have been like a thin brown skeleton autumn leaf dancing eternally before the wind; but in truth it was he that was the wind."

Hurt people are not drawn to the aggressively healthy, to the televangelist's plummy voice, the fire-hose gush of bonhomie. People are instinctively drawn to Jesus, certain that he understands suffering, their particular suffering, that he sees it in their eyes even before they speak. God's chosen are the suffering ones, whose inner luminescence is emphasized by the fragility of its container. The idea that Jesus was a great athlete or captain of industry or persuasive salesman does not square with the fact that he was too weak to carry his own cross, though that was a normal part of the penalty of crucifixion (Lk 23.26). Pilate was surprised that he died so soon, before either of the two men executed with him (Mk 15.44). In Shusaku Endo's novel *Silence*, a Portuguese priest hunted for practicing a forbidden religion in seventeenth-century Japan has been driven alone on a path where he finds no rest or food. As he leans over a muddy puddle, a face stares up at him from the water. He has earlier said how he was consoled in his seminary days by the beautiful Jesus painted by Piero della Francesca. But now he sees a shocking sight, the face of a man haunted and fainting, with a dirty smear of stubble across it. He does not know, but Endo makes us know as we read the passage, that he is looking into the face of Jesus.

I think the least convincing image of Jesus is a macho one, a tough guy, impassive like John Wayne. Wayne did not cry, as Jesus does on two occasions in the gospels (Lk 20.41, Jn 11.35). Even when he towers in wrath, as in the cleansing of the Temple, this is the breathtaking explosion of the man not easily aroused, the searing sincerity that does not depend on muscles to impress. Nothing stuns others more than the sudden eruption of a normally quiet man.

Picture him, then, a man with the future in his eyes, quiet in his mystery, paradoxically calming and provoking others—a Jesus whom Flannery O'Connor described as "the ragged figure who moves from tree to tree in the back of one's mind." This is the man who intrigued other members of John the Baptist's company:

The next day John was again at his post, with two of his followers as he watched Jesus pass by. "That," he said, "is the lamb of God." When the two followers heard him say this, they followed Jesus. Turning his head and seeing them, he asks, "What do you want?" They answer, "Rabbi (which means teacher), where are you staying?" He says, "Come and see." So they went with him, saw where he was staying, and remained with him the rest of the day. (It had been around four o'clock.) One of the two who had heard what John said and followed Jesus was Andrew, Simon Peter's brother. He at once seeks out his brother, the same Simon, and tells him, "We have found the Messiah" (which means the Anointed). He took him to Jesus. (Jn 1.36–42)

One by one, at first, Jesus gathers a select company. Though he is opposed to war and violence, he is choosing followers for a form of spiritual warfare (a metaphor Saint Paul will use): "I come not imposing peace; I impose not peace, but the sword" (Mt 10.34). The drama of this recruitment reminds me of the way King Alfred gathers a (far different) warrior band in Chesterton's "Ballad of the White Horse":

> For I go gathering Christian men
> From sunken paving and field and fen,
> To die in a battle, God knows when,
> By God but I know why.

Jesus tells them little at the outset about who or what he is. He tells them what they will be—that the fishers among them will fish for men (Mt 4.19), that Peter will be called Stone (Jn 1.42), that Nathaniel will see the heavens open (Jn 1.51).

Peter was intrigued by what his brother said of the Baptist's protégé. But what made him a firm follower was a scene that resonates to this day. Early in his teaching, Jesus was pressed up against the lake by a crowd. Seeing Peter's boat lying empty, he asked to go into it, and preached from it as it floated just off the shore. When he finished his discourse, he asked Peter to put out into the lake and do some fishing. Peter assured him they had just finished that work, without result. But Jesus insisted. "Go out to deep water for a great catch" (Lk 5.4). When they pulled in fish so abundantly that other boats were summoned to land them, Peter fell on his knees and said, "Keep away from me, Lord, since I am a sinner" (5.8). Such awe is natural in the presence of Jesus. Some power too good for one's own company is moving in their midst. But Jesus continually tells people, to their astonishment, that no company is beneath his presence. And what he said to Peter he says to all of us. "Go out to deep water." Break away from the humdrum. Bring in unexpected riches.

It is less what he says than what he does that draws men to him. People of a transcendent holiness appear first in a blaze of the miraculous. The legend precedes the fact, with Francis as with the Baal Shem Tov. The very presence of Jesus is cleansing. At a time when sick people were unclean, and therefore were thought to have devils in them, Jesus accepts and nurtures the afflicted, bringing them back into the human community.

The Unclean

HE WALKS THROUGH social barriers and taboos as if they were cobwebs. People and practices other men were required to shun he embraces with an equanimity that infuriates the proper and observant in his culture. Menstruating women, for instance, were unclean and had to be purified before they could go to the Temple. They could not deal with others— prepare their food, wash their clothes—without contaminating them. Thus the woman of Luke's gospel (8.43), who had a perpetual flow of menstrual blood, was a perpetual outcast. She was denied a spiritual life more completely than would those people be who lay under a later church's interdict. According to Leviticus 15.25–27:

> When a woman has a prolonged discharge of blood at the time of her menstruation, or when her discharge continues beyond the period of menstruation, her impurity shall last all the time of her discharge; she shall be as unclean as during the period of her menstruation. Any bed on which she lies during the time of her discharge shall be like that which she used during menstruation, and everything on which she sits shall be unclean as in her menstrual uncleanness. *Every person who touches them shall be unclean; he shall wash his clothes, bathe in water, and remain unclean till evening* [emphasis added].

In order to forbid contact with Samaritan women, Jews claimed that they perpetually menstruated.

For twelve years the woman of the gospel had borne this curse, making endless fruitless appeals to doctors and purifiers of the unclean. Now, desperate for a cure, she defies the ban on contact with others. She jostles through a crowd that presses in on Jesus, reaching out her hand for the edge of his cloak. He turns with a start and asks, "Who touched me?" Though she felt the flow stop instantly, she is afraid to admit that she violated the taboo against contact. Everyone in the crowd denies touching him, and Peter says there is no telling who could have brushed up against him in the press of so many about him. But Jesus insists: "Someone touched me. I realized it when power surged from me" (Lk 8.46). The woman, trembling with fear, throws herself down before him and admits her offense. But he is not offended. He says, gently, "Your trust, my daughter, is what healed you—go in peace" (8.48). Trust, not ritual water, cleanses.

This was not the only unclean woman Jesus allowed to touch him. In the very house of a reproachful Pharisee, he praises a woman of ill repute who anoints his feet (Lk 7.39–50). Even when his friend Mary anoints his feet, he is being touched by an unclean woman, since she lets down her hair to dry his feet (Jn 12.3), and letting down one's hair in public makes a woman unclean, as does any deliberate dishevelment before others (Num 5.18). When Judas rebukes the woman, Jesus says she is doing it as a foreshadowing of his anointment in death, when he will be an unclean corpse (Jn 12.7).

Jesus does not work miracles for their own sake, and he rebukes those who ask him to do so (Mt 12.39, 16.4, Mk 8.12, Lk 11.16). His miracles are targeted to teach lessons about the heavenly reign he brings with him, and one of the main lessons is that people should not be separated into classes of the clean and unclean, the worthy and the unworthy, the respectable and the unrespectable. He has told his followers that they are privileged, since they enter into a new intimacy with the Father through his own identification with the Father. But if they try to make that a privilege to be used against others or each other, they are betraying the point of their union with the Father, whose love is undiscriminating and inclusive, not gradated and exclusive.

"Love your enemies and pray for those who afflict you, so you may be children of your Father of the heavens, who orders the sun to shine on the bad as well as the good, and sends rain on the just and the unjust."
(Mt 5.44–45)

His followers are not to aspire to the social register, but to seek out the forsaken.

"When you give a repast or a meal, do not invite your friends or brothers or relatives, or rich neighbors who may invite you back and repay the favor. When you offer hospitality, call in the poor, the lacking, the lame, the blind, and you will be happy in the fact that they cannot repay you. Your repayment will come when the just shall rise." (Lk 14.12–14)

Many of Jesus' miracles are worked for outsiders—for non-Jews like the centurion (Lk 7.9) or the woman from Tyre (Mk 7.29) or the leper from Samaria (Lk 17.16). But the greatest category has to do with people who are unclean, with whom observant Jews are to have no dealings—with lepers, with prostitutes, with the crippled, with the reviled, with the uncircumcised, or with those made unclean by their illnesses (therefore "possessed"). He tells his followers to call to their feasts "the poor, the maimed, the lame, the blind" (Lk 14.13). He casts the uncleanness out of one man into forbidden animals, into pigs (Mk 5.13), to show that no person made in God's image should be treated as unclean.

Jesus and his followers are themselves called unclean, since they mix and dine with the unclean (Mt 9.10, Mk 2.15, Lk 5.30, 15.2, 19.7). Even when they were not dining with the unclean, the followers of Jesus were unclean because they did not perform the required ablutions before meals (Mt 15.2, Mk 7.2, 7.5). Jesus himself did not cleanse himself before eating (Lk 11.38). Opposed to all formalism in religion, he is willing to challenge the entire "holiness code" of his time. "Understand what you hear from me: What a man takes into his mouth does not make him unclean. What comes out of his mouth—that is what can make him unclean" (Mt 15.10–11). Purity comes from within, from the heart: "Make sure your inner light is not a darkness. If your whole body is suffused with light, no part of it is left in darkness, it will be light-giving, as when a lamp lights you with its brightness" (Lk 11.35–36). The first followers of Jesus would carry the same message. When Christians are called unclean because uncircumcised, Peter defends them by saying, "God, the reader of hearts, testified to their cleanness when he gave the Holy Spirit to them as well as to us [the circumcised]. He made no distinctions between us, since he cleansed their hearts with trust" (Ac 15.8–9). The contrast with the externals of religious observance is stark, and starkly drawn:

"Dire is your plight, Scribes and Pharisees, you pretenders. You cleanse the outside of cup and dish, while the inside teems with larceny and lust. Blind Pharisee, cleanse first the inside of your cup, then the outside will be clean. Dire your plight, Scribes and Pharisees, so like whitewashed tombs, fair to external appearance, but inside all bones of the dead and every filth. Just so are you observant on the outside, where men can see, while inside you are all pretense and exceptions to the Law." (Mt 23.25–28)

Are Some Still Unclean?

No outcasts were cast out far enough in Jesus' world to make him shun them—not Roman collaborators, not lepers, not prostitutes, not the crazed, not the possessed. Are there people now who could possibly be outside his encompassing love? It has been thought so by some Christians. One of the greatest sins of Christianity was to treat Jews as cursed, unworthy of contact, unclean, to be repudiated, in a grisly caricature of their own laws of purification. If this sin of "racial purity" did not cause the Holocaust, it certainly facilitated it.

Who are the Jews of our day? Who are the cursed? Some Christians tell us who. At the funeral of a well-known gay man who died of AIDS, a "Christian" group showed up with placards saying "God hates fags." In the San Diego diocese, a Catholic bishop forbade Christian burial to an openly gay man. Is there any doubt where Jesus would have stood in these episodes—where, in his mystical members, he *was* standing then? He was with the gay man, not with his haters. This is made all the clearer by the fact that gays are called unclean for the same reason as were other outcasts of Jesus' time—because they violate the Holiness Code of the Book of

Leviticus. The anthropologist Mary Douglas has demonstrated that this concept of the unclean comes from the "unnatural" mixing of different kinds of things—of milk and meat, for instance. Examples are planting two different kinds of seed in the same field, or mingling two kinds of yarn in the same garment (Lev 19.19), or ploughing with a donkey and an ox (Deut 22.10), or eating meat with the blood in it (Lev 19. 26).

In the case of homosexuality, the passive partner mixes with his male body the female role. In the Holiness Code, women are unclean anyway, because of their menstrual function. But this fictional "woman" who cannot menstruate is even more unclean. Those who have been anxious to keep this taboo alive in our time are selective in what parts of the Holiness Code they continue to observe from the Book of Leviticus. That is the point of a letter I was shown that came from the Internet (source unidentified—I would be grateful to anyone who can inform me on this). The letter is addressed to a Protestant evangelical who believes in literal reading of the Bible:

Thank you for doing so much to educate people regarding God's law. I have learned a great deal from you, and try to share that knowledge with as many people as I can. When someone tries to defend the homosexual lifestyle, for example, I simply remind them that Leviticus 18.22 clearly states it to be an abomination—end of debate. I do need some advice from you, however, regarding some other elements of God's laws and how to follow them.

1. Leviticus 25.44 states that I may possess slaves, both male and female, provided they are purchased from neighboring nations. A friend of mine claims that this applies to Mexicans but not Canadians. Can you clarify? Why can't I own Canadians?

2. I would like to sell my daughter into slavery, as sanctioned in Exodus 21.7. In this day and age, what do you think would be a fair price for her?

3. I know that I am allowed no contact with a woman while she is in her period of menstrual uncleanliness (Lev 15.19–24). The problem is: how do I tell? I have tried asking, but most women take offense.

4. When I burn a bull on the altar as a sacrifice, I know it creates a pleasing odor to the Lord (Lev 1.9). The problem is my neighbors. They claim the odor is not pleasing to them. Should I smite them?

5. I have a neighbor who insists on working on the Sabbath. Exodus 35.2 clearly states he should be put to death. Am I morally obligated to kill him myself, or should I ask the police to do it?

6. A friend of mine feels that even though eating shellfish is an abomination (Lev 11.10), it is a lesser abomination than homosexuality. I don't agree. Can you settle this? Are there degrees of abomination?

7. Leviticus 21.20 states that I may not approach the altar of God if I have a defect in my sight. I have to ad-

mit that I wear reading glasses. Does my vision have to be 20/20, or is there some wiggle room here?

8. Most of my male friends get their hair trimmed, including the hair around their temples, even though this is expressly forbidden by Leviticus 19.27. How should they die?

9. I know from Leviticus 11.6–8 that touching the skin of a dead pig makes me unclean, but may I still play football if I wear gloves?

10. My uncle has a farm. He violates Leviticus 19.19 by planting two different crops in the same field, as does his wife by wearing garments made of two different kinds of thread (cotton/polyester blend). He also tends to curse and blaspheme a lot. Is it really necessary that we go to all the trouble of getting the whole town together to stone them (Lev 24.10–16)? Couldn't we just burn them to death at a private family affair, like we do with people who sleep with their in-laws (Lev 20.14)?

I know you have studied these things extensively and thus enjoy considerable expertise in such matters, so I am confident you can help. Thank you again for reminding us that God's word is eternal and unchanging.

Some Christians have created a newer holiness code in terms of "natural law." Since the natural end of sexual intercourse is procreation, and gays cannot beget natural children with each other, they say homosexuality is always a sin. This is not so much a case of unnatural mingling as of unnatural disjunction (of sex from procreation). But that meant that late-antique Christians had to say the same thing for heterosexuals—i. e., that sex without procreation is a sin. That was the teaching of Augustine and others. Sex for the sterile, for women beyond menopause, or in infertile periods—all that was forbidden, along (of course) with premarital or extramarital sex, masturbation, coitus interruptus, and anal sex. None of those practices was procreative.

The trouble with this view of the natural is that the primary function of human acts is not normally said to be the only nonsinful use. Eating, for instance, is primarily an act of self-preservation. But much eating and drinking goes beyond that, not only for pleasure but for comradeship, celebration, hospitality, and love. The critics of Jesus noticed how often he used such banqueting symbols—they called him, in fact, a glutton and a drunkard (Lk 7.34). His image of heaven's reign is that of a feast, where no need for subsistence will be at stake.

Why is sex as human communion different from feasting and drinking as human communion? In one way only— because sex is considered unclean. The Christian religion showed that was its view when it created an elite, as opposed to the radical egalitarianism of the gospel, and made the proof of that elite's holiness an abstinence from sex. The priests, the nuns, the holy virgins, the hermits, the desert fathers were considered to be following a higher morality than ordinary married Christians. To them were applied the words of Matthew 19.12: "Some castrated men come so from their mother's womb, others are castrated by men, and some have castrated themselves for heaven's reign. If a man can yield [*chōrein*] to this, let him yield." This passage is distorted in many ways by those who cite it. For one thing, they make a euphemistic translation ("become eunuchs") of the verb for castrating.

The context is set by those saying that Jesus' teaching on marital fidelity is too hard for men to follow. By insisting that internal purity is something more important than externals, Jesus says exactly what he said about the loss of purity through actions of the eye or the hand:

> "You have heard the command, Commit no adultery. I, however, tell you this: One looking at a woman with desire for her has already committed an adultery of the heart. If your right eye makes you fall, rip it out and cast it away. It is better to lose one part of your body than for all of it to be cast into hell. If your right hand makes you fall, chop it off and cast it away. It is better for you to lose one part of your body than for all of it to be cast into hell." (Mt 5.27–30)

Jesus is not calling to an elite to have a standard different from others, but saying that those in danger of sinning are better off suffering physically rather than spiritually.

The idea that Jesus is talking about celibacy, not castration; and that he is talking about celibacy as a higher calling than marriage, to be practiced by the heroes of the faith, is simply absurd. You cannot apply that kind of sophistry to the passages on the right eye and the right hand. What would "celibacy" mean there—not ripping out the right eye, but keeping it closed for life? Nor chopping off the right hand but keeping it in one's pocket for a lifetime? The fact that Jesus is mocking external purity may be hinted in his stress on chopping off the right hand, which was the pure hand for ritual purposes. Similarly, referring to castration may reflect that the castrated were considered unclean (Deut 23.1). Paul makes a savage reference to castration when he says that those still insisting on circumcision for Gentiles "should just castrate themselves" (Gal 5.12).

Jesus called married men to be his emissaries. The most representative of the emissaries, Peter, traveled with his wife even after Jesus' resurrection, as did Jesus' brothers and "the rest of the emissaries" (1 Cor 9.5). Peter's marriage, then, was a model for other husband-and-wife preaching teams—Prisca and Aquila (where the woman is named first, as head of the mission), Andronicus and Junia (who are both called emissaries—*apostoloi*), Philologus and Julia (Rom 16.3, 7, 15). The church of Paul's time was still free of the false later teaching that sex is unclean. Its ministers could, and usually did, marry, like Peter. When Paul refrained from marriage, it was not because sex was unclean but because the End Time was near. He said he preferred "on my own, not from the Lord" (1 Cor 7.12), that the unmarried should stay as they are—as should slaves and the ruled (1 Cor 7.24). Despite all Jesus' efforts, his self-professed followers keep on creating categories of the unclean.

3. The Radical Jesus

Wealth

FOR CREATING RADICALS, there is nothing like a reading of the gospels. They constantly inveigh against the rich, the powerful, the exploiters. "Happy you who are poor, for heaven's reign is yours. . . . But dire your plight, you who are rich, for your time of comfort is over" (Lk 6.20, 24). The young man who has observed all the Law and wants to follow Jesus turns away in sadness "because his possessions were great" (Mk 10.22). Jesus says, when the young man is gone, "It will be hard for those with possessions to enter into God's reign." This perturbs his followers, but he repeats and strengthens his warning: "Little ones, it is very hard to enter into God's reign. It is easier for a camel to get through a needle's eye than for a rich man to enter into God's reign" (Mk 10.23–25).

When a man asks Jesus to defend his property rights against his brother, Jesus replies, "Take care to protect yourself against every desire for having more, for life does not lie in the abundance of things one owns" (Lk 12.15).

Then he tells the parable of the rich man who worked

hard piling up wealth with the intention, someday, of relaxing and enjoying what he had gathered in:

> "But God told him: 'Foolish one, this very night they come to take your life from you. Then all you have accumulated will be—whose?' Such is the lot of one hoarding good things for himself, not becoming rich in God's eyes." Then he told the followers: "This is why I tell you, have no worry for your life, what you will eat, or for your body, what you will wear. Life is a greater thing than what feeds it, and the body is greater than what it wears. . . . Sell all you own and give what it yields to the poor. Use purses that never fray, make investments that never dwindle—in heaven. There no thief can steal it, no moth eats at it. Real wealth will be safe only where your heart is." (Lk 12.20–23, 33–34)

Over and over the gospels tell us that the forces arrayed against Jesus are conditioned by the ownership of property. "When the Pharisees heard what he was saying, they belittled him, attached as they were to riches" (Lk 16.14). Jesus explains why wealth is at odds with the life he brings the world: "No servant can obey two lords. Either he will hate the one and love the other, or pamper the one and scant the other. You cannot serve both God and Greed" (Lk 16.13). This is where Jesus tells the story of Dives ("The Rich Man") and Lazarus:

"Once there was a man of wealth, dressed in soft and purple raiment, enjoying splendid comforts every day. A beggar named Lazarus lay helpless at the rich man's door, covered in sores and hoping to be filled by anything falling from the rich man's table—and dogs licked his own sores. In time the poor man died, and was taken by angels to Abraham's bosom. Then the rich man also died, and he was buried; and when he lifted his eyes from the tortures he was undergoing in Hades, he saw Abraham far off, and Lazarus in his bosom. And he cried: 'Father Abraham, pity me, send Lazarus to dip his finger in water and moisten my tongue as I suffer in this great fire.' But Abraham answered: 'Son, recall how you reaped only goods in life, while Lazarus reaped evils. Now he has this comfort while you suffer. There is, moreover, a vast gulf between us and you, so that none may cross over, from us or from you, however he may want to.' He answered: 'Then, Father, I beg you, send him to my father's house, where I have five brothers. Let him warn them, lest they too come to this place of torment.' Then Abraham says: 'Moses they already have, and the prophets. They should heed them.' He answered: 'No, Father Abraham, but they would heed one returning to them from the dead.' But he answered: 'If they ignore Moses and the prophets, they will not listen even should one return from the dead.' " (Lk 16.19–31)

The one rich man who finds favor during Jesus' ministry is the chief tax collector, Zacchaeus—and that is just because he not only gives away half his wealth to the poor but also makes restitution to all those he has cheated (Lk 19.8). Jesus does not ask him to give up his post at the head of the tax collection service, since he has treated all tax collectors as scorned ones, not beyond his mercy: "The Son of Man has come to seek out the lost and rescue him" (Lk 19.10). Besides, Jesus would be taking a political position if he condemned those who collect taxes for Rome. As we shall see, he avoided all direct political action.

If Jesus demands from his followers in general that they give up the pursuit of wealth, he demands this even more stringently from those who will spread his message. When he sends out his followers, he not only forbids them to take any money with them, they are not even to take along a pack bag *(pēra)* to store something in for the next day. They are to live from day to day entirely dependent on what others will give them: "Take no gold, silver, or copper in your pouch, nor any bag for travel, nor a second cloak, nor sandals, nor a staff. A workman must deserve to be supported" (Mt 10.9–10).

It was in response to passages like this in the gospels that the "worker priests" of France began, after World War II, to live with the people they meant to serve. A similar impulse led to the work of "base communities" in Latin America, where the life of the church was to be seen as the life of the poor. But the gospels are felt as a deep threat to the institutional church. When Saint Francis embodied the radical poverty of the gospel, authorities supported those who would tame the Franciscans and make them conform to more "normal" religious life. Thus the worker priests had to be crushed—by Pope Pius XII. And the base communities were closed—by Pope John Paul II, who took Pius XII as his ideal. Gilbert Chesterton said that Christianity has not failed—it has just never been tried. But when it is tried, it is seen as a threat, just as Jesus was. Churches resist all radicalism— which means that they resist Jesus. They pay lip service to the poor, while distancing themselves from the poor. They do not reflect enough on the obvious—that Jesus wore no gorgeous vestments. He neither owned nor used golden chalices or precious vessels. He had no jeweled ring to be kissed.

Power

THOUGH THE GOSPELS make it clear that riches are the enemy of the spirit, they raise an even more urgent warning against power, and especially against spiritual power. Repeatedly Jesus rebukes the followers who jockey for authority over each other and over others. When asked who will be greater in God's reign, he says, "Whoever becomes as lowly as this child here will be the greatest person in the heavens' reign; and whoever welcomes any child like this in my name, that person is welcoming me" (Mt 18.4–5). Again, when they argued over their own precedence, he said, "Whoever would be first must become the last of all and the servant of all" (Mk 9.35). The guiding rule for a follower of Jesus is to avoid high rank: "For everyone lifting himself up will be abased, and anyone abasing himself will be lifted up" (Lk 14.11). There could not be a clearer injunction against hierarchy of any kind. "The last will be first, the first will be last." His instruction on this matter has been cited earlier:

> "Do not be called Rabbi, since you have only one teacher, and you are all brothers. And call no one on earth your father, since you have only one Father, the one in heaven. And do not be called leaders, since you have only one leader, the Messiah." (Mt 23. 8–10)

Above all, Jesus attacks the arrogance of the spiritual leaders of his time. There is no reason to think this was a special attack on the Jewish religion. He would apply the same standards to every religion, including the ones later invoking his name. All three ranks of spiritual leadership of his time were arraigned by Jesus—the noble and priestly Sadducees, the zealous Pharisees, the learned Scribes. He scorches them. He flays them.

> Then Jesus told the crowds and his followers, in these words: "The Scribes and Pharisees sit in the chair of Moses. You should do as they tell you, and do it scrupulously. But do not do what they themselves do. For they

do not do as they say. They strap together heavy loads, hard for carrying, and place them on men's shoulders; but they would not use a single finger to budge such a load. All their deeds are performed for show in men's eyes. They enlarge their phylacteries and lengthen their tassels. They affect the first table at a feast, the first chair in the synagogue, being saluted on the street and hailed as 'Rabbi.' . . .

"Dire is your plight, Scribes and Pharisees, you pretenders, since you seal up men's access to the heavens' reign, neither entering yourself nor letting others enter.

"Dire your plight, Scribes and Pharisees, you pretenders. You devour the inheritance of widows, stringing out long prayers, which just increase your condemnation.

"Dire your plight, Scribes and Pharisees, you pretenders, who scour sea and land to acquire one adherent, and then you make him twice as fit for hell as you are. Dire your plight, blind leaders. . . .

"Dire your plight, Scribes and Pharisees, you pretenders, who tithe for every piece of mint or dill or cumin, yet do not observe the more important aspects of the law, justice and mercy and trust. It is the latter you should observe, without neglecting the former. Blind leaders, you filter out the gnat but swallow the camel whole." (Mt 23.1–7, 13–16, 23–24)

Jesus was never afraid to speak truth to power. In fact, as we have seen, he addressed the most revered men of his day, the elders and chief priests of the Temple, this way: "In truth I tell you, tax collectors and prostitutes are entering God's reign before you" (Mt 21.31). The complement to that fact is what he told his followers: "In truth I tell you, unless your integrity surpasses that of the Scribes and the Pharisees, you may not enter into the heavens' reign" (Mt 5.20).

It was the pride and ostentation of power that Jesus rebuked in spiritual leaders:

"Two men went to the Temple to pray, one a Pharisee, the other a tax collector. The Pharisee, standing tall, prayed thus: 'God, I thank you that I am unlike the rest of men, thieves, criminals, adulterers, and that I am not like this tax collector here. I fast twice a week, and pay tithes on all I acquire.' But the tax collector, standing at a distance, did not try so much as to lift his eyes to heaven, but he beat his breast and said, 'God, have mercy on me, a sinner.' This man, I tell you, and not the other, went home reconciled to God." (Lk 18.10–14)

Even when Jesus was not openly denouncing the powers of his day, many of his parables were aimed indirectly at undermining their pretensions—as they realized: "When the high priests and Pharisees heard his parables, they recognized that he was describing them" (Mt 21.45). They knew what Jesus meant. He meant *them*.

Of course, Jesus did not condemn all Sadducees, Pharisees, and Scribes. Some Pharisees defended him (Lk 13.31). One of them, Nicodemus, quietly sought his direction (Jn 3.2). Some Scribes, too, joined with Jesus (Mt 8.19), and he speaks of a wise Scribe at Matthew 13.52. In the Acts of the Apostles we learn that certain Pharisees were part of the early church (Ac 5.343, 15.5), and a large number of priests joined his followers (Ac 6.7). These men obviously saw beyond the formalisms of worship.

Egalitarianism

THE OPPOSITE OF HIERARCHY is equality, and Jesus was a radical egalitarian. The early church reflected this value, as we can see from the hymn that Paul quotes:

> Baptized into Messiah
> you are clothed in Messiah,
> so that there is no more
> Jew or Greek,
> slave or free, man and woman,
> but all are one, are the same
> in Jesus Messiah. (Gal 3.26–28)

The equality of men and women was a thing so shocking in the patriarchal society of Jesus' time that his own male followers could not understand it. "At this point his followers arrived, and were thunderstruck [*ethaumazon*] that he was speaking to a woman"—and a Samaritan woman at that (Jn 4.27).

It was a source of scandal for women to travel openly with a rabbi; but "many" women followed Jesus through Galilee (Lk 8.2–3). For a long time the story of Martha and Mary, the latter praised because she sat at Jesus' feet instead of helping Martha in the kitchen, was treated as praise of the contemplative over the active life (Lk 10.38–42). It was used for the practice of sealing women away in convents, which were not far from the kitchen in many cases but certainly were far from "the world." But Jerome Nerey, after a close study of social conditions in Jesus' time, shows that Jesus was defending the woman who would be criticized in his era for acting outside her condoned space, entering the world of the learned (signified by sitting at the feet of a teacher). So, far from closing women into a safe retreat from the world, he was beckoning them out into it, to join men in knowledge and action.

There was a crowd of women followers at the cross, when all but one of the male company had fled or stood far off (Mk 15.40–41). Three of these women who were at the cross were also the first to discover the empty tomb and to announce their finding to the male followers, becoming the first evangels of the Resurrection (Lk 24.1–11). One of these women was the first person to converse with the risen Jesus (Jn 20.15–17).

Women continued to play a prominent role in the early

gatherings. They were prophets (1 Cor 11.5). Paul addresses them as leaders in the various gatherings he formed— Chloe in Corinth, where she speaks for "her establishment" (1 Cor 1.11); Phoebe, the manager *(diakonos)* at Cenchreae (Rom 16.1); Apphia at (probably) Colossae (Phlm 2), where Nympha was also a leader (Col 4.15) At Philippi, Eunoe and Syntyche "struggled by my side for the gospel" (Phil 4.3). Lydia, the dealer in fabrics, led a whole group of women instructed by Paul (Ac 16.13) Other women are mentioned as partners in missionary activity. Junia is called an emissary *(apostolos)*, Paul's own title for himself. She and her husband shared Paul's imprisonment (Rom 16.7). Prisca and her husband are "my fellow workers, who risked their own necks to save my life," so that the whole assembly owes the two of them its gratitude (Rom 16.3–5). Paul refers to four women— Mary, Tryphaena, Tryphosa, Persis—as having "toiled with effort" *(kopiaein,* Rom 16.6, 12) for the Christians, the same verb he uses of his own activities (Gal 4.11, 1 Cor 15.10).

It is clear that women played a much more active role in Christian gatherings than in Jewish synagogues of the time. Though prominent men and women are saluted in the body of Paul's letters, no one is addressed in the honorifics and titles for a leader of synagogues *(archisynagōgos)* or of pagan gatherings *(archōn).* The letters are sent to the whole community, where functions are specified by the gifts of the Spirit, not appointment to an office. Some women are hailed as heads of households, which means that they were the hosts of the Christian meal (agape), a role that would later be restricted to male priests (there are no priests in the Pauline communities). A first-century fresco in the catacomb of Saint Priscilla in Rome shows a woman breaking the eucharistic bread for six other women at the agape table.

The original gatherings of Jesus, still reflecting his teaching, made up the most egalitarian earthly society then in existence. This egalitarianism, combined with Jesus' injunctions against acquiring personal wealth, led the first Christian community to a form of primitive communism, reflecting the common purse maintained among the followers of Jesus (Jn 12.6, 13.29). This was, of course, a voluntary community activity, not state socialism of any kind (Jesus had no political program):

In the company of believers there was a single heart and spirit. Not one of them claimed sole ownership of property. It was all shared—such was the force of the emissaries' witness to the resurrection of Lord Jesus, and the divine favor was over them all. No one was poor with them. Owners of farms or houses sold them and brought the proceeds to lay them at the feet of the emissaries, to be distributed to others according to their need. A Levite from Cyprus, Joseph by name (but renamed by the emissaries Barnabas, which means Son of Support), was the lord of an estate; but he sold it and

brought the profit to lay at the feet of the emissaries.
(Ac 4.32–37)

This has often been called an impossible dream of society,
though communities reading the gospels have, over the
years, lived up to the dream—Eastern monks, the first Franciscans, the Shakers, Catholic Workers, worker priests, base
communities, and Christian communes like Jonah House.

Such people are called dreamers or idealists. Practical
matters require prudence. Jesus does not deny that. Politics,
calculation, compromises—all those things are "matters of
Caesar." Let Caesar take care of them. But that is not the concern of Jesus. His work and demands are of a different order.

Violence

IF JESUS OPPOSED wealth and power, hierarchy and distinctions, he must have opposed their invariable instrument, violence. And of course he did. More than any other
teacher of nonviolence—more than Thoreau, than Gandhi,
than Dr. King—he was absolute and inclusive in what he
forbade:

> "I say to all you who can hear me: Love your foes, help
> those who hate you, praise those who curse you, pray
> for those who abuse you. To one who punches your

cheek, offer the other cheek. To one seizing your cloak, do not refuse the tunic under it. Whoever asks, give to him. Whoever seizes, do not resist. Exactly how you wish to be treated, in that way treat others. For if you love those who love back, what mark of virtue have you? Sinners themselves love those who love back. If you treat well those treating you well, what mark of virtue have you? That is how sinners act. If you lend only where you calculate a return, what mark of virtue have you? Sinners, too, lend to sinners, calculating an exact return. No, rather love your foes, and treat them well, and lend without any calculation of return. Your great reward will be that you are children of the Highest One, who also favors ingrates and scoundrels. Be just as lenient as that lenient Father. Be not a judge, then, and you will not be judged. Be no executioner, and you will not be executed. Pardon, and you will be pardoned. Give, and what will be given you is recompense of crammed-in, sifted-down, overtoppling good showered into your lap. The excess will correspond to your excess." (Lk 6.27–38)

Tremendous ingenuity has been expended to compromise these uncompromising words. Jesus is too much for us. The churches' later treatment of the gospels is one long effort to rescue Jesus from his "extremism." Jesus consistently opposed violence. He ordered Peter not to use the sword, even to protect his Lord (Mt 26.52)—yet thousands, in the Crusades, would take up the sword to protect the site of that Lord's death. If one cannot use violence to protect the Lord, what can one justifiably use it for? When Pilate asks if Jesus is a king, he answers:

> "My reign is not of this present order [*kosmos*]. If it were of this present order, my ministers would do battle to prevent my surrender to the Jews. But for now my reign is not of this present order. " (Jn 18.36)

Many would like to make the reign of Jesus belong to this political order. If they want the state to be politically Christian, they are not following Jesus, who says that his reign is not of that order. If, on the other hand, they ask the state simply to profess religion of some sort (not specifically Christian), then some other religions may be conscripted for that purpose, but that of Jesus will not be among them. His reign is not of that order. If people want to do battle for God, they cannot claim that Jesus has called them to this task, since he told Pilate that his ministers would not do that.

Jesus, unlike other Jews of his time, renounced theocracy. That involves religion in state violence, and he never accepted violence as justified. He specifically renounced political opposition to the Roman oppression, saying "Caesar's matters leave to Caesar" (Mk 12.17). He did not oppose pay-ing the Roman tax, though he was accused of doing that (Lk 23.2). But then people ask how there can be a Christian politics if Jesus renounces "Caesar's matters." The answer is that Jesus did not come to bring any form of politics.

Preparedness

POLITICS IS A MATTER of preparing for the good of the temporal order, and Jesus had a twofold attitude toward preparedness—blithe toward the things of tomorrow, severe toward those of eternity. On matters of earthly provision, he was happy-go-lucky:

> "That is why I tell you this: Do not worry about living, how you will eat or drink, or about your body, what you will wear. Is not your living more than what you eat, your body more than what it wears? Look up at birds in the sky—they do not plant seed, or harvest crops, or collect the harvest in barns. Your Father in heaven tends them. Are you not more precious than they? Who of you by worry can add a foot to his height? And why worry about what you will wear? Take a lesson from the lilies, how they spread over the field. They do not toil at it, they do not spin their own fabric. But I tell you that Solomon in all his splendor did not outshine them. And if God clothes this way the plants of a day, to be thrown on the fire tomorrow, will he not outdo that for you, so

little in your trust? So ask not in your worry, What will we eat? What drink? What wear? That is for the heathen to be bothered with. Your Father knows all the things you need. Seek but God's reign and your right standing with him, and all those things will be provided. So worry not about tomorrow. Tomorrow will take care of itself. Today's problems are enough for now." (Mt 6.25–34)

But he was very exacting when it came to being prepared for heaven's reign. Those who are not prepared for it are guests who lack wedding attire (Mt 22.1–10), or those who neglect the invitation to a feast (Lk 14.15–24), or maidens who do not have oil for their lamps to greet the bridegroom (Mt 25.3–13), or those who did not seek the narrow door (Lk 13.22–30). All such people will be excluded from heaven's reign.

What are the tests for entry into the reign or exclusion from it? They are very simple. One will not be asked whether one voted, whether one was a good citizen, or even whether one dealt justly. That is not enough. Do what is really asked and all else will follow. The simple test is this. Did you treat everyone, high and low, as if dealing with Jesus himself, with his own inclusive and gratuitous love, the revelation of the Father's love, whose sunshine is shed on all? Love is the test. In the gospel of Jesus, love is everything. But this love is not a dreamy, sentimental, gushy thing. It is radical love, exigent, searing, terrifying:

"When the Son of Man comes in his splendor, with all his angels about him, he will sit on the throne of his splendor, and all peoples shall be gathered before him, and he will separate them as a herdsman separates his sheep from his goats, and he will station the sheep on his right hand, and the goats on his left hand. Then the Ruler will tell those on his right hand: 'Approach, you blessed of my Father, take possession of the reign prepared for you from the cosmic origins. For I hungered and you gave me food. I thirsted and you gave me drink. I was an alien and you welcomed me, I was naked and you clothed me, I was ill and you tended me, I was in prison and you came to me.' Then the vindicated will respond to him: 'Lord, when did we see you hungry and we fed you, or thirsty and we gave you drink? When did we see you as an alien, and we welcomed you, or naked and we clothed you? When did we see you ailing and we tended you, or in prison and we went to you?' And the Ruler will reply, saying: 'In truth I tell you, whenever you did these things to the lowliest of my brothers, you were doing it to me.' Then he will say to those on his left hand: 'Off from me, with a curse on you, to the eternal fire prepared for the devil and his angels. For I hungered and you fed me not, I thirsted and you gave me no drink. I was an alien and you welcomed me not, I was naked and you clothed me not. I was ill and imprisoned and you tended me not.' Then they will respond to him: 'Lord, when did we see you hungry or thirsty or alien or naked or ill or imprisoned and we did not care for you?' Then he will reply, saying: 'In truth I tell you, whenever you failed to do these things to the least of my brothers, you failed to do it to me.' And they will go off to eternal punishment, while the vindicated go to eternal life." (Mt 25.31–46)

What exactly does that mean? "Whenever you did these things to the lowliest of my brothers, you were doing it to me." It means that priests who sexually molest boys are molesting Jesus. Televangelists who cheat old women of their savings are cheating Jesus. Those killing members of other religions because of their religion are killing Jesus. Those who despise the poor are despising Jesus. Those neglecting the homeless are neglecting Jesus. Those persecuting gays are persecuting Jesus. And that judgment of his is being delivered now, at the moment when he is scorned, ignored, left hungry. He is outcast, and we welcome him not. He needs us, and we do not take up his cross with him, love with him, die with him. That is the awesome test of love that Jesus brings to bear on our lives. Admittedly, Jesus was an extremist, a radical, but can any but radicals justly claim his name?

4. Against Religion

THE MOST STRIKING, resented, and dangerous of Jesus' activities was his opposition to religion as that was understood in his time. This is what led to his death. Religion killed him. He opposed all formalisms in worship—ritual purifications, sacrifice, external prayer and fasting norms, the Sabbath and eating codes, priesthoods, the Temple, and the rules of Sadducees, Pharisees, and Scribes. He called authentic only the religion of the heart, the inner purity and union with the Father that he had achieved and was able to share with his followers:

"When you pray, be not like pretenders, who prefer to pray in the synagogues and in public squares, in the sight of others. In truth I tell you, that is all the profit they will have. But you, when you pray, go into your inner chamber and, locking the door, pray there in hiding to your Father, and your Father who sees you in hiding will reward you. And when you pray, do not babble on as the pagans do, who think to win a hearing by the number of their words. Your Father knows what you need before you ask it of him." (Mt 6.5–8)

This inner religion is not less demanding of the worshiper, but more demanding. It calls for a radical cleansing of the heart not to be achieved by externals:

"You have heard the command, Commit no adultery. I, however, tell you this: One looking at a woman with desire for her has already committed an adultery of the heart. If your right eye makes you fall, rip it out and cast it away. It is better to lose one part of your body than for all of it to be cast into hell. If your right hand makes you fall, chop it off and cast it away. It is better for you to lose one part of your body than for all of it to be cast into hell." (Mt 5.27–30)

As with his other teachings, his followers could not understand Jesus on this matter of inner purity. Even as he neared death, when he tried to set the pattern of menial service as the mark of his life, Peter was obtuse. When Jesus did observe the ablution before meals, Peter said that Jesus could not stoop so low as to wash his followers' feet. In his typically peremptory tone, Peter informed Jesus: "Never will you wash my feet" (Jn 13.8). But when Jesus insisted, Peter flipped to the other extreme: "Then not my feet alone, but my hands and head as well." Jesus says he is missing the point—that the intention, the inner state of service being signaled, is what matters, not the external ritual:

> "Can you not see what I have done for you? You salute me as teacher and Lord, and you speak aright. That is what I am. But if I, your teacher and Lord, wash your feet, surely you should wash each other's feet. This was a pattern I gave you, that as I acted with you, so should you with each other; for I tell you, the servant is not greater than his master, nor an emissary greater than the one who dispatched him." (Jn 13.12–16)

As Jesus went to the inner truth of the purity code, so he went to the inner truth of the Sabbath, where he rejected niggling legalities.

The Sabbath

TRAVELING ABOUT on the Sabbath (itself a violation), Jesus' followers, forbidden to carry money or supplies, eased their hunger by picking and cleaning ears of corn. "The Pharisees, seeing this, said, 'What of this—your followers do what is forbidden on the Sabbath?' " (Mt 12.2) Jesus gives two answers, one topping the other in defiance. In the first, he compares himself to David. In flight from Saul, with famished troops, David and his men ate the Bread of the Presence from the Temple, which was not supposed to be eaten except by the

Temple's priests, even when removed from the Presence. David said his men were made sacred by their mission (1 Sam 21.1–6). In his second answer, Jesus assumes an authority greater even than David's:

> "Are you unaware that by law the priests on the Sabbath break Sabbath law in the Temple and are not blamed? Yet I tell you that here we have something greater than the Temple. If you grasped the meaning of 'It is mercy I desire, not sacrifice,' you would not have condemned the blameless. The Son of Man is Lord over the Sabbath." (Mt 12.5–8)

In Mark's report of this incident, Jesus says, "The Sabbath exists for man, not man for the Sabbath" (Mk 2.27).

Jesus repeatedly "breaks" the Sabbath by doing work on it—the work of healing. He defends himself this way: "If one of you had only one sheep, and it fell into a pit on the Sabbath, would you not grapple and haul it out? How much more is a man worth than a sheep? The Sabbath does not forbid rescue" (Mt 12.11–12). Jesus especially offends the authorities when he heals on the Sabbath while actually teaching in a synagogue (Lk 13.11–12). On another occasion he tells a cripple, after curing him, to carry his pallet on the Sabbath (Jn 5.8). Jesus himself violated the ban on productive work when he took earth and spittle on the Sabbath and mixed a paste from them to put on a blind man's eyes (Jn 9.6–7). It should be remembered that the Book of Exodus gives the penalty for doing work on the Sabbath as death (31.15).

Jesus proves that even the sticklers for the law do manual work (surgery) on the Sabbath. Since male circumcision was mandated for the eighth day after birth, a boy born on the Sabbath had to be circumcised on the succeeding Sabbath:

"You are all shocked at this single work I have done. Moses prescribed circumcision for you (though it dates not from Moses but from the patriarchs), so you circumcise a male on the Sabbath. If a male can be circumcised on the Sabbath, to avoid violating the law of Moses, why do you fume at me for making the whole man well on the Sabbath? Judge not by outer appearance, but use sound judgment." (Jn 7.21–24)

Sacrifice

JESUS CRITICIZES not only the formalisms of the purity code and the Sabbath, but the whole Temple ritual of animal sacrifice. "Go off and discover what is meant by 'I desire mercy and not sacrifice' " (Mt 9.13). Jesus is referring to 1 Samuel 15.22: "Obedience is better than sacrifice, and to listen to God is better than the fat of rams." Jesus cites the same text at Matthew 12.7. He could have appealed to many texts in the Psalms and prophets to show that a religion of the heart is preferable to one of external observances. As God says at Hosea 6.6: "Loyalty is my desire, not sacrifice, not whole-offerings but the knowledge of God." And Psalm 51.16–17 says:

> Thou hast no delight in sacrifice;
>> if I brought thee an offering, thou wouldst not accept it.
> My sacrifice, O God, is a broken spirit;
>> a wounded heart, O God, thou wilt not despise.

Jesus had a great Jewish tradition to invoke in his criticism of certain religious leaders of his time. No wonder Jesus approves of the lawyer who puts the whole Law in this brief statement: "There is one God, and next to him are none. And to love him with one's entire heart, entire mind, and entire effort, and to love one's neighbor as oneself—that is more important than any kind of burnt offering or sacrifice" (Mk 12.32–33). This is the religion of the heart.

It is sometimes said that Jesus does not attack animal sacrifice when he drives from the Temple precinct those trading in the animals of sacrifice and the money involved in their purchase, since he says only that these hucksters have turned "my Father's house" (the Temple itself) into a traders' mart (Jn 2.16) or thieves' lair (Mk 11.17). But his action stops sacrifice itself. The money changers take Roman coins with their graven images and trade them for shekels that can be used to pay Temple dues, and the sale of doves and other animals supplies the means of sacrifice. By preventing sacrifice, Jesus attacks the whole sacrificial system, which he sees as corrupted and corrupting. He cites and fulfills prophecies of the end of the Temple. First he cites Isaiah (56.7): "Was it not written, 'My house shall be known as a house of prayer *for all peoples?*' " (Mk 11.17, emphasis added). Then he refers to Jeremiah:

"You keep saying, 'This place is the Temple of the Lord, the Temple of the Lord, the Temple of the Lord.' This catchword of yours is a lie; put no trust in it. . . . You come and stand before me in this house, *the house which bears my name,* and say, 'We are safe'; safe, you think, to indulge in all these abominations. *Do you think that this house, which bears my name, is a robbers' cave?* I myself have seen all this, says the Lord. Go to my shrine at Shiloh, which once I made a dwelling for my name, and see what I did to it because of the wickedness of my people Israel. And now you have done all these things, says the Lord; though I took pains to speak to you, you did not listen, and though I called, you gave no answer. Therefore what I did to Shiloh I will do to *this house which bears my name,* the house in which you put your trust, the place I gave to you and your forefathers. I will fling you away out of my sight, as I flung away all your kinsfolk, the whole brood of Ephraim." (Jer 7.4, 10–15, emphasis added)

Jesus' action in the Temple says that this prophecy is being fulfilled. The Temple is doomed, it will be destroyed.

Jesus makes his meaning clear by cursing the fig tree that bore no fruit just before his interruption of the Temple service, and then by noticing the effect of the curse on the fig leaves just after the interruption (Mk 11.12–14, 20–21). The bracketing of his Temple action in these two stages of a parallel symbol fulfills another prophecy in Jeremiah:

"Are they ashamed when they practise their abominations? Ashamed? Not they! They can never be put out of countenance. Therefore they shall fall with a great crash, and be brought to the ground on the day of my reckoning. I would gather their harvest," says the Lord, "but there are no grapes on the vine, no figs on the fig tree; even their leaves are withered." (Jer 8.12–13)

When his followers marvel at the effect of his curse on the fig tree, Jesus immediately adds:

"Have faith in God. In truth I tell you that should one tell this mountain [the Temple mount], 'Rise from your place and be flung into the sea,' and doubts not in his heart but believes that what he says is done, so it will be for him. That is why I tell you that when you ask for something in prayer, believe it is done and it will be." (Mk 11.22–24)

The Temple mount is flung away, just as in Jeremiah's prophecy. Jesus is replacing it with inner faith and the religion of the heart.

Priests

IF JESUS DISAPPROVED of the sacrificial system, it is not surprising that the high priests managing that system should fear and resent him. Jesus was a layman, like the Jeremiah who said, "All, high and low, are out for ill-gotten gain; prophets and priests are frauds, every one of them" (Jer 6.13). In the gospels, priests are the most active plotters to kill Jesus. They think not only that he is committing blasphemy but also that he is undermining their livelihood. They conspire to assassinate him (Lk 19.47) and also to kill the risen Lazarus (Jn 12.10). They reward Judas for betraying Jesus (Mt 26.14–15). They petition Pilate to set a guard on his tomb (Mt 27.62–64). Their action has nothing to do with the later libel that all Jews were "Christ killers." They show how all religious formalists have reason to fear Jesus—a fact of Christian history as well as of Jewish. One truth is hidden

deep in Dostoyevsky's fiction about the desert temptations—
that the Christian Inquisition repeatedly executes Jesus: "Whatever you did to the lowliest of my brothers, you were doing
it to me" (Mt 25.45).

Given the hostility between the priests and Jesus, it is not
surprising that there are no priests among his followers. The
word *hiereus* is not used of any Christian in the four gospels
or the Pauline letters. Jesus calls no one that. Paul does not
call himself or his coworkers that, or any of the people he addresses in the gatherings he founded. There are many ministries referred to in the New Testament. Paul mentions
thirteen in the First Epistle to the Corinthians—emissaries
(apostoloi), prophets, teachers, miracle workers, healers, as-
sistants, guides, speakers in tongues, interpreters of speakers
in tongues (12.27–28), wise men, interpreters of wisdom,
spirit testers (12.8–10), and trainers (*paidagogoi*, 4.15). He
gives a shorter list at Romans 12.6–8, which however adds
four other roles—stewards *(diakonoi)*, exhorters, distributors
(metadidontes), patrons, and almsgivers. He adds two more
at Ephesians 4.11—evangelists and shepherds—making nine-
teen ministries in all, none of them priestly or episcopal.

These are all functions, not offices, and they derive from
the Spirit, not from human organization or any bureaucracy
(1 Cor 2.11–16). They are not regulated or reduced to a
hierarchy. It is a strictly charismatic community that Paul
knows—and remember that he writes anywhere from twenty

to fifty years before the gospels, giving us our earliest picture of how the first followers of Jesus acted. There are outstanding men and women in the communities, but they are given informally descriptive terms by Paul, like "pillars" of the church (Gal 2.9)—and some of these Christian eminences he describes sardonically as "the super-too-much emissaries" (*hoi hyperlian apostoloi*, 2 Cor 11.5).

What is striking in terms of later developments, but perfectly understandable in terms of Jesus' relationship with the priesthood of his day, is that this early church functioned entirely without priests. As I say, Paul never calls himself or anyone else a priest. The closest he comes is in his letter to the Romans, where he says he is "a minister [*leitourgos*] of Jesus Christ among the foreigners, giving priestly devotion [*hierourgoun*] to God's revelation" (Rom 15.16). His word for minister *(leitourgos)* is used, in the same letter, for secular officials (13.6). The verb *hierourgein* refers to his devoted service to the revelation—that is, to his announcement of the crucified and risen Jesus as God's son (his regular description of "the gospel"). This does not have any connection with a sacrificial office, which was the meaning of priest in his time.

Nowhere is it indicated that there was an official presider at the Christian meal (agape), much less that consecrating the bread and wine was a task delegated to persons of a certain rank. It is a mark of the gospels' fidelity to the followers' original status that not one of them mentions a Christian

priest or priesthood. When the term "priesthood" finally occurs, in the pseudo-Petrine letters, it refers to the whole
Christian community (1 Pet 2.5, 2.9), and the "Peter" of this
letter refers to himself not as a priest but as a "fellow elder"
(sympresbyteros) to the other elders *(presbyteroi, 5.1)*, urg-
ing them to perform their tasks devoutly. He is "an elder,"
not even the first of the elders:

> I encourage you elders as a fellow elder, one who saw
> what Christ suffered, sharing with you the splendor
> that is coming, be you shepherds to God's sheep, not du-
> tifully but gladly in God, not as grasping at gain but
> giving freely, not as lording it over them but as setting
> an example. Then when the Great Shepherd comes, you
> will receive the unfading crown of splendor. Young peo-
> ple, in your turn, follow the lead of the elders, so that all
> wear a livery of humble service to the others, since God
> baffles the lofty but favors the lowly. (1 Pet 5.1–5)

Those final antihierarchical words show that the early church
remembered the Jesus who said, "Call no one on earth your
father, since you have only one Father, the one in heaven"
(Mt 23.9). The elders of the pseudo-Pauline "pastoral letters," the highest functionaries of the gatherings in the early
second century, have no sacramental functions and are presented as model family men over the households where
Christians gather. They must be sober and not greedy, with

only one wife, and their children must be not only Christian but also well behaved (Titus 1.6, 1 Tim 3.2–5). There are still no priests in the gathering.

The only Christian priest mentioned in the New Testament is Jesus himself, who is called that in only one place, the Letter to the Hebrews, where it is said that he is the last priest, who makes other priesthood obsolete (Heb 7.28, 9.12, 10.12). The letter does not speak of anyone who follows him as sharing or continuing or perpetuating his priesthood. It is unique to him.

Temple

SINCE THE JEWISH PRIESTHOOD existed for adoration and sacrifice at the Temple, Jesus thought that the priesthood was no longer necessary because the Temple was about to become unnecessary. He revealed this to a woman who, as a Samaritan, did not worship at the Temple in Jerusalem but at her dissident region's temple at Gerizim. The enmity between the other Jews and the Samaritans was made clear in 128 B.C.E., when the high priest from Jerusalem burned down the Gerizim temple. Because of their heresies, Samaritans were treated as unclean by the Jerusalem Jews—yet one of the lepers Jesus cured was a Samaritan (Lk 17.16). That man was, therefore, doubly unclean until Jesus healed him.

Jesus expressed his sympathy with the Samaritans by telling the story of a Samaritan traveler who helped a critically injured man after a high priest and a member of the priestly tribe (from the class that had destroyed the Gerizim temple) passed him by (Lk 10.30–36). The injured man seemed almost dead, and the Leviticus code said that touching a dead man made one unclean. That is why the text uses a rare double compound verb to say that the observant Jews "went-past-far-off" *(antiparēlthon)* the injured man—they were avoiding contamination. The story of the "good Samaritan" is often told simply to show goodness of heart in the rescuer. It also shows the inhuman effects of the purity code of the Jewish priesthood. The story is a powerful part of Jesus' attack on the formalisms of "religion."

Jesus makes his sympathy with the Samaritans even clearer by his address to the Samaritan woman. He has defied convention by traveling to the very base of the temple mount in Samaria—and this despite an earlier rebuff when he tried to travel through Samaria: when it was clear that he was going to the Temple in Jerusalem, the Samaritans told him not to use their territory for such a purpose. Jesus' indignant followers wanted to call down fire on the stubborn schismatics, but Jesus checked them: "The Son of Man is here not to take men's lives but to rescue them" (Lk 9.56)—a point he reemphasizes in the story of a Samaritan, of all people, as a rescuer. Here, then, with the woman at the well, Jesus has again breached Samaritan territory, this time successfully, since he is not traveling toward the Temple.

He breaks another taboo by opening a conversation with an unclean woman. He increases his offense, in the eyes of the observant, when he reveals that he knows this is a woman of ill repute, even beyond her schismatic status—she has been five times married and is now living with a man not her husband. Despite all this, he shows compassion to her, and she recognizes in him "a prophet." Their conversation turns at first on ritual cleanness. He has asked that she dip her bucket and draw him some water from the deep well. She hesitates, since she knows that he as a Jew is supposed to consider the water unclean if she handles the bucket. He tells her that he is bringing a water that cannot be defiled, the "living water" of inner purity, "a spring within bubbling up to life everlasting" (Jn 4.14). The life he brings does not depend on external cleansings.

Then he goes to the root of the estrangement between the Samaritans and other Jews, their dueling holy mounts:

"Believe me, the moment is coming when you will worship the Father neither on this mountain [Gerizim] nor in Jerusalem. Here you worship without understanding, while we worship with understanding, since rescue comes from the Jews. The moment is coming, and is now here, when true worshipers will worship the Father in Spirit and truth—and those are the worshipers the Father seeks [not ones who worship through external formalities]. Since God is Spirit, his worshipers must worship in Spirit and truth." (Jn 4.21–24)

The woman says that for this to be true, the Messiah must come. Jesus answers. "I am he, I who tell you this" (Jn 4.26).

This is just one of the places where Jesus says that he will replace the Temple as the site for encountering the Father. The Anglican bishop and Bible scholar N. T. Wright thinks that this puzzling parable also refers to the Temple:

> "An unclean spirit, ousted from a man, wanders the barren places seeking a rest, but finds none. He says then: 'I shall return to the house from which I was expelled.' On his return he finds the house empty, swept out and put in order. And he goes out to get seven other spirits more vicious than itself, who return with him and make it their house. And worse is this later state of the man than before. That is how it will be with this vicious generation." (Mt 12.43–45)

The "house" referred to, says Wright, is the Temple, which was "cleaned and put in order" by the Maccabees (1 Mac 4.36–51) and later reformers, only to have it revert to even worse abuses as the years went by.

At the Temple, only priests were allowed into the Holy of Holies, where God was a disembodied Presence. All have access to Jesus, who is the moving Path to the Father. He is God's self-manifestation to men, his Word spoken to them. "I tell you that here we have something greater than the Temple" (Mt 12.6). When Jesus drives the merchants out of the Temple, onlookers challenge him: "What authorization [sēmeion] can you produce for doing this?" He responds: "Destroy this Temple and in three days I will raise it again." The Jews scoff at the mere idea of rebuilding the Temple in three days: "Construction of the Temple has taken forty-six years." But the gospel adds: "The Temple he referred to was his body" (Jn 2.21).

The Temple of Jerusalem was destroyed by the Romans in 70 C.E., and it never rose again. But Jesus had already loosened it from its moorings, to float off into the religious past, replacing it with his own inner religion, centered in himself as the embodiment of the Father's love. The priests were bound to see blasphemy in his words about the Temple, words which would be used against him at his trial (Mt 27.40, Mk 15.9). But it would be wrong to see in this an attack on the Jewish religion itself. He told the Samaritan woman, "We [Jews] worship with understanding, since rescue comes from the Jews" (Jn 4.22). But he is bringing a new stage of religion—all religion—one not based on externalities and foreshadowings, but on the revelation of the Father in Jesus.

He would have the same reaction he had to the profanation of the Temple if he walked into Saint Peter's Basilica in Rome—or, for that matter, into the Mormon Tabernacle or

Robert Schuller's Crystal Cathedral. Jesus had said, after all, that his followers should not "lord it over others" like the pagan kings (Lk 22.25). They should not be like rabbis who "affect the first seat in the synagogue" (Lk 11.43). "And do not be called teachers, since you have only one teacher, the Messiah. The greater among you will be a servant. The one lifting himself up will be abased, the one abasing himself will be lifted up" (Mt 23.10–12). Yet in Saint Peter's he would look at a huge blazon of gold and jewels around Bernini's apotheosis of "Saint Peter's Chair," to which the whole vast basilica is a shrine. Saint Peter himself had shown an obtuseness on the externals of religion when Jesus appeared transfigured before him, in a vision that included, at the outset, Moses and Elijah. Yet those two figures withdraw, leaving only Jesus as the fulfillment of their prophetic roles (Lk 9.32). Peter wants to build three booths of worship because, Luke says, "he spoke without knowing what he was talking about" (Lk 9.33).

Jesus did not come to replace the Temple with other buildings, whether huts or rich cathedrals, but to instill a religion of the heart, with only himself as the place where we encounter the Father. At first one might think that Jesus would not recognize most of what calls itself religion today. But, on second thought, it would probably look all too familiar, perpetuating the very things he criticized in the cleanliness code, the Sabbath rules, the sacrifices, and the Temple. It was natural, therefore, for religion to kill him, since he was its foe.

His followers would be killed for the same reason. Stephen, the first martyr, is stoned for predicting the destruction of the Temple (Ac 6.14). Stephen tells his executioners what Jesus told the Samaritan woman: "The Most High does not live in houses constructed by human hand. Rather, as the prophet says, 'Heaven is my throne, and earth my footstool' " (Ac 7.48–49).

What is the kind of religion Jesus opposed? Any religion that is proud of its virtue, like the boastful Pharisee. Any that is self-righteous, quick to judge and condemn, ready to impose burdens rather than share or lift them. Any that exalts its own officers, proud of its trappings, building expensive monuments to itself. Any that neglects the poor and cultivates the rich, any that scorns outcasts and flatters the rulers of this world. If that sounds like just about every form of religion we know, then we can see how far off from religion Jesus stood.

5. Heaven's Reign

Did Jesus Found a Church?

BUT WAIT A MINUTE. Didn't Jesus found a church? The first works of the New Testament have Paul writing to Christian "churches" two decades after Christ's death. The Greek word usually translated "church" is *ekklēsia,* a "gathering"—a word that occurs in only one gospel (Matthew's). It is used for a mob at Acts 19.32, 40. The gatherings that Paul addresses are those nonhierarchical bodies already described. He does not write to a leader of the community but to the gathering, in which there are no priests. Nor are there churches in our sense—that is, church buildings. The gatherings meet at houses (*oikoi,* 1 Cor 1.16, 16.19, Rom 16.5, Phlm 1.2, Col 4.15, Ac 11.14, 12.12). This is such a standard thing that Paul could talk of Christians in general as "house-gatherers *(oikeioi)* of the faith" (Gal 6.10).

These stable groups are not led by "apostles." That word means someone "sent off" (from *apo-stello*), an emissary from one community to another—Paul equates being an apostle with being an ambassador (*presbeutēs,* 2 Cor 5.20, Eph 6.20). Thus Peter and Paul, as apostles, are simply emissaries to the gathering in Antioch—by contrast with James, the Lord's brother, who is not an apostle but is one of the "pillars" of the Jerusalem gathering (Gal 2.9).

It is a common error to think of apostles as the Twelve (plus Paul, since he calls himself an apostle without having been one of the original Twelve). But in two of the four gospels, the Twelve are called only the Twelve, and in the third (Luke) they are normally called that. When the gospels refer to "the twelve apostles" (Mt 10. 2), this marks the point when *they* are expressly "sent out" on a temporary mission to other Jews during Jesus' public ministry (that is, formally as emissaries). Elsewhere "apostles" is a broad term for many "emissaries" (1 Cor 15.7), including the woman Junia (Rom 16.7). The Twelve, by contrast, have a distinct prophetic and eschatological role, to preside over the reunion of the Twelve Tribes of Israel. When Peter asks what reward he and his fellows will have for leaving everything to follow Jesus, he gets this answer:

> "In truth I tell you, you who have followed me will, at the Restoration, when the Son of Man sits on his throne of splendor, sit on your own twelve thrones judging the twelve tribes of Israel. And any person who left brothers or sisters or father or mother or children or fields or home for my honor will have many times the profit, as well as eternal life, while many of the first will be last, and the last first." (Mt 19.28–30)

That antihierarchical last sentence shows that the symbolic-prophetic meaning of the Twelve has nothing to do with church governance below. The passage confirms what the Catholic priest and biblical scholar John Meier concludes, that Jesus gave his movement no authority structure.

But what about Peter? Did not Jesus found his church on Peter, and give him the keys of the Kingdom? Well, Peter is clearly the leading member of the Twelve. But he, like all other apostles or disciples, is not a priest—much less a bishop. There were no bishops in his lifetime, and none in Rome till the second century (as the letters of Ignatius of Antioch prove). As we have seen, he calls himself just one of the elders—not a priest, nor the first of elders—in the letter attributed to him (1 Pet 5.1). The Catholic scholar Raymond Brown wrote, "Peter never served as the bishop or local administrator of any church, Antioch and Rome included."

But didn't Jesus say he was founding a church on Peter? The words are these: "You are Peter [*Petros*], and on this stone [*petra*] I will build up my gathering [*ekklēsia*]. And I will give you the keys of heavens' reign. Whatever you tie on earth will have been tied in heaven, and whatever you loose on earth will have been loosed in heaven" (Mt 16.18–19). But Jesus in the same gospel gives the same power not to Peter exclusively but to the followers as a body: "In truth I tell you [*hymin*, plural] that whatever you tie on earth will have been tied in heaven, and whatever you loose on earth will have been loosed in heaven" (Mt 18.18). From this Augustine concluded that Peter is just "a representative of the church"—and in fact the community as a whole had the power to include or exclude members in the early gatherings.

Peter's qualification is not that he is the wisest, steadiest, or strongest of the followers—he is far from that. He is favored as the woman of ill repute was: "Her great sins are forgiven her, as her great love shows" (Lk 7.47). So Jesus forgives Peter his triple denial by asking three times, "Simon Peter, do you love me more than all else?" (Jn 21.15–17). The idea that Peter was given some special power that could be handed on to a successor runs into the problem that he had no successor. The idea that there is an "apostolic succession" to Peter's fictional episcopacy did not arise for several centuries, at which time Peter and others were retrospectively called bishops of Rome, to create an imagined succession. Even so, there has not been an unbroken chain of popes. Two and three claimants existed at times, and when there were three of them, each excommunicating the other two, they all had to be dethroned and the Council of Constance started things over again with a new appointment in 1417.

Yet Pope Benedict XVI, when he was still Cardinal Ratzinger, the head of the Congregation for the Doctrine of the Church, wrote in 1998 that it is an infallible teaching of the church that Anglican bishops and priests are fake bishops and priests, dispensing fake sacraments, because they are outside the apostolic succession. That is, they have not a lineage guaranteed by papal elections, supposedly guided by the Holy Spirit—a line in which bribery, intimidation, and imperial interference were often the deciding factors. In this famous succession, the papacy was often bought, and once was sold for money (by Benedict X). Popes were for a long time appointed by various temporal rulers. Popes were heretical (Liberius, Honorius), they waged wars, they ran governments (with their full complement of armies, spies, and torturers), and they granted indulgences for those killing heretics (the Albigensians) or infidels. This succession is what excludes saintly Christians of non-Catholic gatherings as not "valid," not connected with the mythical chair of Peter as bishop of Rome.

Jesus said, "Where two or three are met together in my name, there am I in their midst" (Mt 18.20). Why do Anglicans, met together in Jesus' name, need a bishop from Rome when they have Jesus in their midst? Benedict XVI's stand brings to mind the disciple John in Luke's gospel:

John said, "Master, we found a man casting out devils in your name, but we stopped him since he was not of our company." But Jesus answered him: "Do not stop him, since anyone who does not oppose you supports you." (9.49–50)

The exclusionary attitude of Benedict is just one example of the way the religion Jesus opposed has taken over the gatherings claiming descent from him. It was a tendency that showed up even in his own lifetime. When a blind beggar called out to Jesus, his followers told him to shut up, but "Jesus halted, and said, 'Call him over' " (Mk 10.49). Or again:

> Some brought children for him to caress; but the followers rebuked them. Jesus, however, saw what was happening, and was angry at it. He said, "Let the children through, do not block them. The subjects of God's reign resemble these. In truth I tell you, whoever does not approach God's reign as a child will not be let into it." And he hugged them, with a blessing as he caressed. (Mk 10.13–16)

Exclusion returned with the reinstitution of a "Christian" priesthood, along with revived holiness codes—consecrated altars and consecrated men and "consecrating fingers," with the extrusion of the laity (especially women) from altars, from secret conclaves, from decision making, from control of the believers' money. The "rood screen" separating clergy from laity was a great barrier in the Middle Ages and it survived for a long time in the "communion railing." Women, returned to the unclean status given them by menstruation under Jewish (and other) law, were not allowed inside the sanctuary of a church—even the altar cloths had to be carried out to the nuns who washed them. For these groups, Jesus cleansed the Temple in vain.

Heaven's Reign

IF JESUS DID NOT COME to establish a church, why did he come? He said it over and over, from the outset. He brought us heaven's (or the heavens') reign. "The announced time is fulfilled, God's reign impends. Turn back, and trust in the revelation" (Mk 1.15, like Lk 10.9–11). The word for "reign" *(basileia)* is normally translated "kingdom," but that is a misleading term. It suggests a place or a political structure. The Christian reign is the personal presence of Jesus. On the one hand, he tells us to ask in the Lord's Prayer that "your reign arrive" (Mt 6.10), and the full arrival will come only at the Eschaton, the world's completion. Yet he also speaks of it as already arrived when the Father's love was revealed in Jesus—at first in his preaching and healings, then in his death, and then in his Resurrection. The New Order of Creation has begun.

He says, during his ministry, "God's reign is in your midst" (Lk 17.21). This has the same meaning as his words in Matthew's gospel, "Where two or three are met together in my name, there am I in their midst" (Mt 18.20). He equates heaven's reign and his personal presence. His miracles are meant to prove this: "If I, with God's touch, cast out devils, then God's reign has arrived" (Lk 11.20). When John's followers ask if Jesus is "the one we hope for"—that is, the Messiah—Jesus gives the signs of the Messiah's arrival: "Blind men see, lepers are cleansed, deaf men hear, and poor men hear the revelation of God" (Lk 7.22). God's announcement, the "gospel" normally translated "good news," is precisely the news that the Messiah has arrived. As Jesus tells the Samaritan woman, the prophesied Messiah is there with her (Jn 4.26). He tells his followers privately, "Happy the eyes seeing what you see. For I tell you many were the prophets and rulers who longed to see what you are seeing, yet saw it not, to hear what you are hearing, and they heard it not" (Lk 10.23–24). "You are privileged to know the secrets of heaven's reign" (Mt 13.11). Thus some are already entering the reign (Mt 21.31). At his last gathering with his followers, he tells them, "Now I give to you the reign the Father gave to me" (Lk 22.29).

Yet God's reign, though present when Jesus announced it, had not completed its triumph. The reign is a dynamic process, not a settled place or structure. It is not two things, one present and one to come. It is one process unfolding. It is Jesus himself, at first recognized only by a few, but extending his hold by fulfilling his mission from the Father. There are stages to be reached—first his death, Resurrection, and exaltation, then his final return to bring the new order to its consummation. Then the whole universe will be fully united with the Father. That is why Jesus can speak of the reign as already among his followers, yet speak as well of their future entry into it (Mt 19.23–26, 20.21–22, 21.43), or of the difficulty of entering (Mk 10.22–25, Lk 18.24–26).

The emergence of the kingdom through various stages is emphasized by the parables that begin, "The reign of God is like . . ." It is like seed sown without result until it lands on fertile ground (Mt 13.18–23). It is like a seed sown without notice, one that springs a surprise (Mk 4.26–29), or like a mustard seed, deceptively tiny but growing to great height in time (Mk 4.31–32, Lk 13.18–19). It is like wheat growing, but with weeds in it, to be separated only at harvest time (Mt 13.25–30). It is like yeast slowly working in the dough (Mt 13.33, Lk 13.20–21). It is like treasure buried in a field, to be taken out only after a man has bought the field (Mt 13.44). It is like a rich pearl, to be purchased only after a man has raised the money for it (Mt 13.45). It is like a king who calls in his debts, taking gradual payments, forgiving those who spare their own debtors (Mt 18.23–35). It is like a landholder who pays at the end of the day, even to latecomers (Mt 20.1–16). It is like a man who invites some to his son's wedding, but brings in others when those invited do not come (Mt 22.1–14). It is like the wedding for which some maidens prepare their lamps, and some do not (Mt 25.1–13). It is like a man who gives his property in care to others while he travels, with the result that some use the property wisely, some do not (Mt 25.14–30).

Nowhere in this process of the growth and revelation of the reign of Jesus is an earthly realm claimed or accepted. In fact, when some try to proclaim Jesus king, he escapes into the hills (Jn 6.15). When Pilate asks if he is king, he answers:

> "My reign is not of this present order. If my reign were of this order my subjects would be fighting for me, to keep me from arrest by the Jews, but for now my reign is not here." (Jn 18.36)

Jesus is telling Pilate that he is not a Jewish rebel trying to end Rome's occupation.

Pilate nonetheless treats him as a political figure, nailing the name of his crime on the cross: "Jesus from Nazareth, King of the Jews." It was said earlier that religion killed Jesus. But so did politics—not his own, but that of the earthly realm that fears unearthly claims. From the time of Herod's panicky response to the birth of Jesus, worldly power has had to fear Jesus, not because he will challenge it for control of a throne or a realm, but because he undercuts its claim to supremacy. The occupiers of Jesus' country claimed the authority stamped on the denarius Jesus refers to at Mark 12.16. That inscription said (in abbreviations), "Tiberius Caesar Augustus, *son of the Divine Augustus.*" His dry remark to

those asking whether they should traffic in such blasphe-
mous coin was "Give to Caesar what he has a right to [that
is, *not* the claim to divinity], but to God what he has a right
to" (Mk 12.17). That is the challenge to earthly power's pretensions that earthly power cannot abide.

The heavenly reign, though it undercuts the earthly
reign's claim to be more than what it is, does not exempt
Christians from the duties of all human beings to be just to
others, according to the rules of temporal conduct. But it goes
far beyond those rules. It treats the lowest person, the outcast person, as if he were Jesus. Those who try to cram this
overriding duty within the structure of any state are making
Jesus a king in Pilate's sense. They follow the lead of Jesus'
enemy, not of Jesus. The program of Jesus' reign can be seen
as a systematic antipolitics. What politician could be elected
on the following platform?

"I say to all you who can hear me. Love your foes, help
those who hate you, praise those who curse you, pray
for those who abuse you. To one who punches your
cheek, offer the other cheek. To one seizing your cloak,
do not refuse your tunic under it. Whoever asks, give to
him. Whoever seizes, do not resist. Exactly how you
wish to be treated, in that way treat others. For if you
love those who love back, what mark of virtue have
you? Sinners themselves love those who love back. If

you treat well those treating you well, what mark of virtue have you? That is how sinners act. If you lend only where you calculate a return, what mark of virtue have you? Sinners, too, lend to sinners, calculating an exact return. No, rather love your foes, and treat them well, and lend without any calculation of return. Your great reward will be that you are children of the Highest One, who also favors ingrates and scoundrels. Be just as lenient as that lenient Father. Be not a judge, then, and you will not be judged. Be no sentencer, and you will not be sentenced. Pardon and you will be pardoned. Give, and what will be given you is recompense of crammed-in, sifted-down, over-toppling good showered into your lap. The excess will correspond to your excess." (Lk 6.27–38)

Anyone claiming to practice a "Christian politics" other than this is a usurper.

Entry into the Reign

HOW DOES ONE ENTER into heaven's reign? Thomas asks Jesus, "How should we find the path [to the Father]?" and he answers: "I am the path, and the truth, and the life. None arrives at the Father but through me" (Jn 14.6). Heaven's reign is, simply, Jesus—finally, when the Father exalts his Son on the throne of judgment, but also now, when the Father's love is to be found only in him. Entering into the kingdom is the act of union with Jesus. This is not a political activity. It is certainly not an action of ecclesiastical politics, of a churchly rule or realm. Jesus was opposed to religion in any sense but this meaning of heaven's reign.

Heaven's reign unites believers with the Father by uniting them with Jesus, who says, "I am in the Father, and you are in me, and I in you" (Jn 14.20). This, and nothing else, is the heavenly reign:

"Remain in me, as I remain in you. As a branch cannot be fruitful on its own, without remaining on the vine, so you can bear no fruit but by remaining in me. I am the vine, you the branches. The one remaining in me, as I in him, will be richly fruitful; but severed from me, you can do nothing. Whoever does not remain in me is like a severed branch that withers, the kind men gather and throw into the fire, where it burns. If you remain in me, and my words remain in you, ask for whatever you desire and it will be given you. My Father's glory consists in this, in your being richly fruitful, in your being my followers. As the Father has loved me, so love I you. Remain in that love. You will remain in it if you follow my instructions, just as I have followed my Father's instructions and remain in his love. I have told you this to make my joy yours, and to complete your joy. This is my instruction: Love one another as I have loved you." (Jn 15.4–12)

One enters the heavenly reign by only one avenue—love. That avenue not only leads to Jesus. It is Jesus. "I am the path" (Jn 14.6). Augustine's words on this verse say it all: "Where should we go but to him? And how should we go but by way of him? So he goes to himself through himself, and we go to him by way of him, and both of us—he and we—arrive at the Father."

6. Descent into Hell

Lazarus

JESUS EMBRACED his own death when he gave life to Lazarus. When he answered the call from Lazarus's sisters, he was going back into the killing zone, as his followers protested: "Rabbi, just now the Jews were trying to stone you, and you are returning there?" (Jn 11.8). When he says he is going anyway, Thomas voices the feelings of the others: "Go we along, then, we too shall die with him" (Jn 11.16). But Jesus did not respond instantly to the request of Lazarus's sisters. John's gospel shows that Jesus waits to act on the Father's timeline for movement toward his "hour." Here at the end of his ministry he acts as he did at its beginning, not responding to his mother's request at the marriage in Cana. He does not work miracles from humanitarian motives. At Cana he worked a disproportionate sign to convince his followers that they were moving toward the fulfillment of history (Jn 2.11). As he begins his last journey to Jerusalem, he tells them the climax to his story is almost at hand:

> Jesus told them, "Daylight lasts only twelve hours, does it not? If a man walks by daylight, he does not stumble,

since he sees by the light of this present order. But if a man walks in the night, he stumbles, since there is no light in his eye." (Jn 11.9–10)

The light is about to go out, when Jesus will say to the priests and elders, "This is your hour, your authority of darkness" (Lk 22.53).

Jesus tells the followers that he goes to "wake" Lazarus. But this is not simply a matter of resuscitating a person on his or her deathbed—as he had done with Jairus's daughter (Mk 5.22–43) or the Nain widow's son (Lk 7.11–17). Lazarus has been dead for four days and is already buried. As his sister says, "Lord, by now, after four days, he must stink" (Jn 11.39). But that is why Jesus did not come at once. He does not come to do a human favor, but to declare his authority over life and death. Before acting, he makes clear to Martha what this event will mean:

Jesus tells her, "Your brother will rise again."

Martha tells him, "I realize that he will rise again at the resurrection on the last day. "

Then Jesus told her, "I am the resurrection and the life. Whoever trusts in me, though he die, will live, and everyone who lives with trust in me will not ever die. Do you have this trust?"

She says to him, "Yes, I have reached the trust that you are the Messiah, the Son of God, the one coming into the world." (Jn 11.23–27)

Jesus, when he proves that he can raise Lazarus, is telling his followers that his own death will be voluntary: "This is why the Father loves me, that I lay down my life in order to take it up again. No one takes it away from me. No, I lay it down on my own. I have the authority to lay down my life and the authority to take it up again. I do this on the direction of my Father" (Jn 10.17–18).

Though Jesus makes this masterly claim, the gospel shows him emotionally wrought as never before as he approaches Lazarus's tomb. The language is strong:

> When Jesus saw her weeping, and the other Jews with her likewise weeping, he was convulsed [*enebrimēsato*] within, and loosed his passion [*etaraxen heauton*]. And he said, "Where have you buried him?" They answer him, "Lord, come and see." Jesus broke into tears, which made the Jews say, "Look at how he loved him." But some said, "Since he opened the blind man's eyes, could he not have kept this man from dying?" But Jesus was once more convulsed [*embrimomenos*] within himself as he approached the tomb. (Jn 11.33–38).

Why, if Jesus knows he can and will raise Lazarus, is he so distraught and tearful? Because his agony has begun. He knows that this conquest of death is part of his own personal struggle with death, with his fear and human dread. He was truly human as well as divine. He knew hunger and thirst, loneliness and pain. He foresaw that he would suffer all these things and more in one hideous tortured end to his life. Those standing around did not understand the implications of his act. John does not report the agony in the garden of Gethsemane. This is his equivalent of it.

The other gospels make the interruption of the Temple service the immediate cause of Jesus' arrest. John put that episode at the beginning of Jesus' ministry, just as Luke put the temptation in the desert at the beginning, as a symbol of the issues that lay behind the entire public ministry of Jesus. For John, the cause of Jesus' arrest is the raising of Lazarus. Just as Jesus had explained to Martha, this was a Messianic act. It proclaimed Jesus as the Lord of life—therefore he must die. He advanced a claim that the Temple priests could not abide. When they heard of crowds flocking to Bethany to talk with the risen Lazarus, they plotted to kill Lazarus (Jn 12.10).

Martin Scorsese, in his film *The Last Temptation of Christ*, presents what the stakes are in the raising of Lazarus. To show Jesus taking on the power of death, he has him reach into the tomb and pull at the hand of Lazarus. But then Jesus is almost pulled into the tomb. Only with great difficulty does he extract the revivifying body. It is, indeed, a symbolic entry into his own tomb that Jesus is undergoing, a struggle at the boundaries of life. In giving life to others, he gives his own life to and for them. This is shown in the gospel by his hesitation to go back to Bethany, his talk with the followers of the darkness approaching, his spiritual convulsion, his tears. It is significant that the only other time Jesus weeps in the gospels is on this same last journey to Jerusalem, when he grieves over the city, when he sees the destruction of its Temple foreshadowed in the obliteration of his own body:

> As he neared the city, he cried tears at sight of it, saying, "If only you could know the things that would give you peace on this day. But it is sealed off now from your sight. The days will come when your foes direct siege works at you, encircling and hemming you in from all sides, leveling you along with your children inside the walls, and they will not leave a stone upon a stone in you, since you knew not the critical moment of your visitation." (Lk 19.41–44)

The last clause refers to Jeremiah's prophecy (in the Septuagint) that "they will perish in the time of their visitation" (Jer 6.15). The Messiah has come to reclaim his city, but its rulers (as distinct from the body of its people) will not be reclaimed:

> "Jerusalem, Jerusalem, you who kill the prophets and stone the emissaries sent you, often I wished to shelter your children to me, as a hen shelters her chicks under her wings, but you would not consent, So, see, your

house is forsaken. And I tell you this, that never again will you see me until you say, 'Acclaim for him who comes in the name of the Lord.' " (Mt 23.37–39)

Messianic Entry

JOHN SAYS that the triumphal entry of Jesus into Jerusalem on "Palm Sunday" was a direct reaction to the raising of Lazarus.

> The crowd, which had been there when Jesus called Lazarus from his tomb and raised him from the dead, was keeping up report of it. That is why a crowd came out to meet him on his entry, because they had heard of his working this portent. This made the Pharisees tell each other, "Look, your actions so far are no use. Everyone has flocked around him." (Jn 12.17–19)

Jesus approached Jerusalem from the Mount of Olives and the Valley of Cidron, like the triumphant Messiah of Zechariah 14.4. He enters the city riding an ass, like the Messiah of Zechariah 9.9–10:

> Rejoice, rejoice, daughter of Zion,
> shout aloud, daughter of Jerusalem;
> for see, your king is coming to you,
> his cause won, his victory, gained,

humble and mounted on an ass,
on a foal, the young of a she-ass.
He shall banish chariots from Ephraim
and warhorses from Jerusalem;
the warrior's bow shall be banished.
He shall speak peaceably to every nation,
and his rule shall extend from sea to sea,
from the River to the ends of the earth.

The expectation created by this and other prophecies was of a military Messiah who would extrude the foreign (Roman) rulers; but Jesus has, from the quietly subversive challenge to Herod as a child, undercut all political contexts. His reign is not of this order, though the Romans and the high priests misunderstand that. He comes as a thief in the night, to steal the dominion from earthly and Satanic powers by a universal solvent of love. The heir to all the promises God had made to Israel is now coming to his own, and his own could not recognize him (Jn 1.11). It was the story Jesus had already sketched in his parable of the vineyard owner:

"There once was a landowner who built for himself a vineyard, raised a wall around it, and fortified it with a tower. Then he rented it to tenants and left the area. When the season for harvest came, he sent his slaves to collect his revenue. But they took hold of the slaves, whipped one, killed one, and stoned one. He sent more servants, in greater force, but they treated them the same way. At last, he sent them his own son, saying, 'My son they will heed.' But as soon as the tenants saw the son, they told each other, 'This is the heir. Quick, let us kill him and get his estate.' They seized him, dragged him out of the vineyard, and killed him. When the owner of the vineyard comes himself, how, do you suppose, will he treat these tenants?" (Mt 21.33–40)

While others were carried away on Palm Sunday by the excitement of the "sign" worked for Lazarus, Jesus knew that the plaudits would turn into shocked and disappointed anger and violence. He rode in a swirl of acclaim to his foreseen degradation, and he rode in fear. John Ruskin noted the irony of Palm Sunday when he saw an ass eating palms in the huge crucifixion scene of Jacopo Tintoretto. The triumph and the defeat are indeed linked, since both are messianic. Not the Messianism of wars and conquest but that of the Suffering Servant in Isaiah 53. The irony of Palm Sunday, the victory of the despised, is expressed in Chesterton's poem "The Donkey":

> When fishes flew and forests walked,
>   And figs grew upon thorn,
> Some moment when the moon was blood,
>   Then surely I was born.
>
> With monstrous head and sickening cry,
>   And ears like errant wings,

The devil's walking parody
  Of all four-footed things.

The tattered outlaw of the earth,
  Of ancient crooked will;
Starve, scourge, deride me: I am dumb,
  I keep my secret still.

Fools! For I also had my hour,
  One far fierce hour and sweet:
There was a shout about my ears,
  And palms before my feet.

Judas

MOST OF THE FOLLOWERS of Jesus are stock figures, so interchangeable that the names of all the Twelve are not certain from gospel to gospel. Only Peter is a rounded person, a character out of Dostoyevsky, impulsive, strutting, cringing, generous, weak, laughable, lovable, bobbing up again as unsinkable as a cork. But one other disciple suggests a person who might figure in modern novels—as indeed he has. Like many other villains, Judas is more vivid than his virtuous fellows. The novelists François Mauriac and Shusaku Endo give special emphasis to him in their biographies of Jesus. Endo and Graham Greene put Judas figures in their novels (*Silence* and *The Power and the Glory*). He has found an out-and-out champion in William Klassen, who expanded his long "Anchor Bible Dictionary" article into a major book on Judas.

There must have been some good in the man for Jesus to have chosen him not only to follow him but to be one of the Twelve and the trusted bearer of the common purse (Jn 13.29). Judas is a practical man, who deplores the waste of money on precious oils, but he seems idealistic as well, wanting to save the money for the poor (Jn 12.4–5). He is the only person Jesus addresses as his "comrade" (*hetairos*, Mt 26.50). He reclines in an honored position near Jesus at the final supper (Jn 13.26). There is an odd complicity between Jesus and Judas, as if they were fencing over the heads of the unwitting disciples. Endo is especially struck by Jesus' whispered words at the Last Supper: "What you are doing, do swiftly" (Jn 13.27), and by his intimate words in the garden, "Why, comrade, are you here?" and "Judas, do you turn over the Son of Man with a kiss?" (Lk 22.48). Jesus knows that Judas is fulfilling the plan of the Father, which leads to the disgraceful death and burial of both men. He says of his followers in general: "Not one of them is lost but the one marked out to be lost to fulfill the scripture" (Jn 17.12). Judas is involuntarily following the will of the Father, as Jesus does voluntarily:

"The Son of Man takes the path marked out for him by scripture. But dire is the lot of him who gives over the

Son of Man. It were best for that man not to have been at all." Judas, who was turning him over, said in response, "Surely, Rabbi, it is not I?" Jesus says, "You say it." (Mt 26.24–25)

Why did Judas sell Jesus? John's gospel says it was for the thirty pieces of silver, since he was "a thief" (Jn 12.6). Most of those who have become intrigued by his story doubt that it was that simple. Mauriac writes, "The miserable calculations of avarice would not have been sufficient to determine him." Since the disciples indulged in "jealous rivalry" (Lk 22.24), he imagines Judas suffering some hurt in his jockeying for Jesus' favor. He wanted justice, not realizing that "love is unjust." Endo rather thinks that Judas' discontent was political, a disappointment that Jesus was not advancing a worldly kingdom (which the disciples had generally favored). Paul Schrader and Martin Scorsese adopt this reading in their film, *The Last Temptation of Christ*.

All these men think that Judas, in betraying Jesus to the high priests, did not believe that he would be sentenced to death, since Jews had no authority for capital punishment under Roman rule. He did not foresee that Jesus could be turned over to Pontius Pilate, who had the power to crucify. They think Judas may have been trying to shock Jesus into taking a more aggressive and rebellious stand against Rome, to convince him that endlessly turning the other cheek would not liberate the land. They imagine that Judas followed with increasing horror the process of Jesus' trial and torture. Endo writes:

> When he saw the figure of the loving Jesus being beaten by everybody, when he saw Jesus spouting blood, he stared at the shift in circumstances in waves of mixed emotion—loathing himself, then excusing himself, hating the master, then loving him.

Some such process would explain Judas' final actions.

> When Judas, who turned him over, saw him condemned, he was overcome with remorse, he returned the thirty silver pieces to the high priests and elders, saying, "I have sinned in turning over this innocent man." But they said, "What do we care? It is your concern." He threw the silver down in the Temple and left it, and went off to hang himself. (Mt 27.3–5)

The money was "blood money," unclean and contaminating the Temple. It could not remain there. So it was taken out to buy a graveyard for burial of the unclean, which Judas as a suicide surely was. Jesus, as a crucified figure, was also unclean and would have to be buried apart from others. Both men ended their shameful deaths in shameful graves.

Judas could not bear the knowledge of what he had done.

He killed himself for having killed God. It was an act of contrition that redeems him, makes him a kind of comrade for all of us who have betrayed Jesus. He is our patron. Saint Judas.

Gethsemane

IN JOHN'S GOSPEL, Jesus was convulsed with emotion and wept when he had to wrestle Lazarus back from death to life. In the synoptic gospels, he is even more desperately racked by emotion when he prays to the Father to escape his coming ordeal:

> They arrive at a place known as Gethsemane, and he says to his followers, "Stay here while I pray." And he takes Peter, James, and John with him. But as he began to feel terrified [*ekthambeisthai*] and helpless [*adēmonein*], he tells them, "I am anguished [*perilupos*] to the point of death. Stay here and keep alert." Going a little farther, he fell on the ground and prayed that, if it were possible, his time might go away. He said: "Abba, Father, you can do all things—yet your will prevail, not mine."
> He comes back and finds them asleep, and says to Peter: "Sleep you, Simon? Not one hour could you stay awake? Keep awake, and pray that you enter not into the Trial [*Peirasmos*]. The spirit is ready, but the flesh fails." Going off again, he prayed. And coming back

again, he found them asleep, since their eyes were heavy, and they could not give an account of themselves.

A third time he returns and says, "Still asleep, still not alert? Let be. The time is come. The Son of Man is turned over to the hands of sinners. Get up and come, my betrayer has arrived." (Mk 14. 32–41)

Elsewhere Jesus emphasizes that he and the Father are one, that his will is a reflection of the one who sent him. But here there is a wedge driven into that deepest union. He would escape the Father's will if he could. He prays, but there is no answer. Heaven is dumb, and earth sleeps. As Mauriac said, "The Son of Man became a pendulum swinging between man's torpor and God's absence—from the absent Father to the sleeping friend." He is entirely alone and deserted. No human despondency will ever equal his.

How, if Jesus was God, could he be deserted by himself? He was both man and God—but fully man. The Epistle to the Hebrews, one of the principal statements of Christ's divinity, says, "He was put to every possible test, just as we are, but without sinning" (Heb 4.15); "He *learned* how to obey from what he suffered and *reached* fullness" (Heb 5.8–9). Just as he underwent thirst and hunger, loneliness and pain, he had to overcome ignorance by learning to read and write (under the handicap of coming from a probably illiterate family). As Luke puts it, "He grew physically and intellectually" (Lk 2.40). What was entailed in the Epistle to the Hebrews phrase that "he learned how to obey" is spelled out in that early hymn already quoted, saying that Jesus

> emptied himself out into the nature of a man,
>> becoming like to man,
> and in man's shape he lowered himself,
>> so obedient as to die, by death on a cross. (Phil 2.7–8)

This emptying is suggested in Luke's description of the scene in Gethsemane: "In his agony, he prayed even more desperately, and his sweat fell in great drops as if he were bleeding" (Lk 22.44). His inner rending wrung from him a sign of the greater ordeal ahead.

Jesus did not wear merely the outer shell or facial mask of a man (as the ancient Docetists taught). He had to enter into the full tragedy of humanity, its bewildered helplessness, its shame, its sense of inadequacy and despair. That is the meaning of the dark cry from the cross saying that even the Father had abandoned him. To experience all the aspects of human contingency, to plumb those depths, is a way of descending into hell.

The repetition of his prayer three times is a scriptural device for showing a prolonged experience, just as Luke did in the desert struggle with Satan. In fact the triple prayer in

Gethsemane, at the end of the public ministry, is a companion piece to the triple trial in the desert. In the earlier experience, Jesus was learning his vocation. In the later one, he fully accepts the consequences of that vocation. Both episodes are emblematic of the stakes being played for in the whole public ministry. They are a way of showing what was going on "behind the scenes," as it were, the high mystery being worked out which even the disciples only dimly witnessed, as they adverted only to the outward surface of meaning. We are taken by Luke into the inner reality of God's purpose, where Jesus wrestles with evil and with himself. The later victory completes the first, against even worse odds. In the desert, at least, his enemy was out in the open, to be faced and fenced with, as Satan voiced the baser temptations. In the last showdown, by contrast, he has no one to speak with, not even the Father. He must conquer himself, all alone, with no human or divine help. All that is nondivine in him must leap into oblivion, fully understanding that that is what he does. Only by being completely crushed as a human can he accomplish the utmost in human heroism.

7. The Death of God

WHY WAS JESUS KILLED? The legal answer to that question
is unequivocal. His crime was announced on the instrument
of his death: "The King of the Jews" (Mk 15.26). Pontius Pilate, who alone had authority to execute Jesus, focused on his
political identity. "Are you the king of the Jews?" That is the
question Pilate asks, in exactly the same Greek words, in all
four gospels. It is the only thing that matters to Pilate. He
must uphold the religious as well as the temporal power of
the deified Caesars. At this basic level it is, once again, religion that kills Jesus—Roman religion, and Pilate's inability
to understand the otherworldly nature of Jesus' kingship.
Paul is firm on this point: "The masters of this age crucified
him" (1 Cor. 2.8).

For Jesus does not deny that he is king of the Jews. In all
three synoptic gospels, when Pilate asks Jesus if he is king
of the Jews, he answers, "So you say" (Mt 27.11, Mk 15.2,
Lk 23.3). That is his messianic title, under which he has initi-
ated heaven's reign. But it is not a title that can be ranked
with or against or at the level of Roman (or any other) im-

perium. Pilate does not know, or want to know, that. A religious kingship is still a kingship in his eyes. Or perhaps something worse. Bishop N. T. Wright has traced the Roman imperial policy of humoring local religious practices only if they were subject to the ideology of the deified Caesars.

> Pilate re-entered the praetorium, and summoned Jesus, and said to him: "You, are you the king of the Jews?"
>
> Jesus replied: "Do you ask this on your own, or did others ask it of me?"
>
> Pilate replied: "You don't take me for a Jew, do you? Your own people and its high priests have given you over to me. What have you been up to?"
>
> Jesus replied: "My reign is not of this present order. If my reign were of this present order, my supporters would have fought against my being turned over to the Jews. But my reign is not here."
>
> Pilate said, "So you are a king?"
>
> Jesus answered: "King is what you call it. The reason for my birth, for my entry into the present order, is simply to be a witness to truth, and anyone open to the truth hears my call."
>
> Pilate says to him: "What is truth?" (Jn 18.33–38)

The fact that Jesus was killed for being king of the Jews was not an afterthought pinned on the cross above his head. The

Roman soldiers commissioned to prepare him for execution knew that was the issue. That is why they gave him the burlesque of a coronation, clothing him in royal purple and giving him a mock crown and scepter before they abased themselves and called out, "Hail, king of the Jews" (Jn 19.1–3). That scene, the clothing of Jesus in spurious emblems of temporal authority, has been repeated down through the centuries by people claiming to be Christ's followers. Christian emperors did this first, both in the East and in the West. Then popes did it. The divine-right kings. Now some evangelical Christians do it. All have dressed Jesus in borrowed political robes. They will not listen to the gospels, where Jesus clearly says that his reign is not of this present order of things. The political power they claim to exercise in his name is a parody of his claims, like the mock robe and crown put on him by the Roman soldiers. These purported worshipers of Jesus are doing the work of Pontius Pilate. Jesus, born on the run from power, is still hunted by it.

The mock crowning was an improvised game of the soldiers—unlike the scourging of Jesus, which was a prescribed part of the sentence of execution on a cross. The flogging was used to reduce the powers of resistance before hanging a man on the cross. The rebellious bandit executed with Jesus no doubt had to be beaten with special ferocity to bring him under control. There was no similar reason to flog the unresisting Jesus in that way. But some assume that he was savagely beaten. They allege as proof the fact, first, that he was too weak to carry his own cross (Lk 23.26) and, second, that Pilate was surprised when Jesus died so soon (Mk 15.44–45). But perhaps Jesus, like so many mystics, was a frail man to begin with—which would lend a special pathos to the ugly ordeal he underwent.

Crucifixion was the cruelest possible act of a generally cruel regime—Cicero called it "the extremest penalty" (summum supplicium). As such, it topped an ascending order of deaths by torture. The least savage was beheading. Above that came lethal exposure to beasts in the circus. Then burning a man alive. And finally crucifixion. The utter shamefulness of crucifixion was such that Roman citizens were normally not subject to it. The tradition that Nero crucified Saint Peter but only beheaded Saint Paul probably comes from the fact that Luke calls Paul a Roman citizen (Ac 16.37–38, 23.27).

Crucifixion involved a whole galaxy of horrors. I wonder if young people consider that when they wear gold or jeweled crucifixes as earrings or necklace pendants. Before writhing on a cross, the condemned man was given a preliminary scourging. Then he had to carry the crosspiece of his instrument of death, tied on his shoulders, to the place where the upright beam of the cross was already fixed in place. Then he was stripped naked, to be tied or nailed to the cross.

Most would today consider nailing the worse ordeal,

though that was not necessarily so. The worst part of crucifixion was the long agony of hanging on the cross, for hours or even for days. Since the nails were driven through the wrists (nails in the palms would not hold a man, his weight would tear through the gap between the fingers), a severed artery could shorten the period of long hanging. The weight of the body constricts the breathing of a crucified man unless the victim pulls himself up with progressively agonizing efforts, and the longer he hangs there the more literally excruciating these efforts become. In Jesus' case, it is said that "doubting" Thomas wished to probe the wound in Jesus' "hands" (Jn 20.24–25)—but this does not contradict the nailing through the wrist, since "hand" is a general term for the arm's extremity. The point is that nails were used.

Crucifixion was also a climactically horrible thing to Jewish minds. It made Jesus, who had treated no one as unclean, as unclean as a person could possibly be—as an accused blasphemer (Lev 24.14), a publicly naked man, a crucified man (a sight offensive to God according to Deuteronomy 21.23), a corpse. The Jews removing Jesus' body from the cross would have to go through ritual cleansings. The courage of the woman who went on the day after the Sabbath to treat this unclean body with respect is particularly estimable. So were the crowds of women who accompanied Jesus to Golgotha (Lk 23.27) and bravely gazed on the unclean sight of Jesus hanging on the cross (Mk 15.40)—when all his male disciples but the Beloved Disciple had fled.

Thus there was only one disciple there into whose care Jesus could give his mother, one of those women standing throughout his exposure, a mother who saw what they were doing to the flesh she bore (Jn 19.26–27).

Jesus, even in his worst extremity of pain, thinks of others besides his mother:

> One of the criminals suspended there was taunting him: "Aren't you the Messiah? Save yourself—and us."
>
> But the other responded, rebuking him: "Have you no fear of God? You are sentenced as he is, and we are getting what our crimes deserve, while this man has done no wrong." And he addressed Jesus: "Remember me when you enter on your reign."
>
> Jesus told him: "This day, with me, you will be in Paradise." (Lk 23.39–43)

This is the last chance Jesus has to reach out to the unclean—for the body of this man will also get ignominious burial, as a cursed and defiling object—yet Jesus will take the man to Paradise with him, for what the poet Denise Levertov calls "the promise given from cross to cross at noon." And it is not only the unclean criminal beside him to whom he extends forgiveness. For those who have made the crucifixion an excuse for racial and other divisiveness, there is a crushing rebuke in Jesus' cry, "Father, forgive them, since they do not know what they are doing" (Lk 23.34). Forgiveness must be widespread since those turned against him were many. He was, in the words of Raymond Brown, "abandoned by his disciples, betrayed by Judas, denied by Peter, accused of blasphemy by the priests, rejected in favor of a murderer by the crowd, mocked by the Sanhedrin and by Roman troops and by all who came to the cross, surrounded by darkness, and seemingly forsaken by his God."

Jesus was plumbing the last depths of the despair he had tasted in Gethsemane: "And on the ninth hour Jesus shouted in a loud voice, *'Eloi, Eloi, lama sabachthani?'* "—in translation, "My God, my God, why have you abandoned me?" As Chesterton says:

> We may surely be silent about the end and the extremity, when a cry was driven out of that darkness in words dreadfully distinct and dreadfully unintelligible, which man shall never understand in all the eternity they have purchased for him; and for an annihilating instant an abyss that is not for our thoughts had opened even in the unity of the absolute; and God had been forsaken of God.

The Deeper Reason

BENEATH ALL THE HORRORS of a Roman execution, there is a deeper question than the legal one, a theological puzzle: Why did Jesus die? A common answer depends partly on Saint Anselm's influential book *Why the Incarnation? (Cur Deus Homo?)*. Using feudal analogies, Anselm argued that Jesus *had* to become man in order to pay God a debt that man could not pay on his own. The offense of original and all subsequent sin was of an infinite nature because the offended party is infinite. Only an infinite spokesperson for man could pay the debt with his life.

But why did the payment include Jesus' death, and such a horrible death? Was the creditor so exacting? Behind this conclusion lies the imagery of an angry God, hard to appease but by the most terrible of sacrifices. This is a view that some people call "gruesome." The philosopher-critic René Girard says that it affirms the violent rituals of sacrifice, which load a society's guilt onto a scapegoat to be punished. Girard argues that Jesus is incapable of assuming guilt, so he exposes the fundamental absurdity of curing violence by violence.

Others question the idea that there would have been no Incarnation without the fall of man. Some Franciscan theologians argue that the Incarnation is the culmination of God's plan from the outset, whereby he raises man to himself in the person of his incarnate son. Creation without that deeper union between man and God would have been incomplete. They draw on some works by the early church father Irenaeus, who called Jesus the "recapitulation " *(anakephalaiō-sis)* of all creation in its glorious end. A Pauline letter signaled something like that:

> His grace is overflowing to us in every kind of wisdom and knowledge, revealing the secret of his purpose, the loving care of his prior arrangements in Christ, that he

bring the stages of all things to their fulfillment, summing them all up [*anakephalaiōsasthai*] in Christ, all
that is in the heavens, all that is on earth. (Eph 1.8–10)

This passage accords with other writings of Paul, where—
as Gordon Fee points out—he does not follow the logic of appeasement sacrifices, where the offending party must initiate
compensation. In Paul, God is like the father of the prodigal
son, who rushes to embrace beforehand, or like the good
shepherd, who searches out his lost sheep. This God does not
sit on a throne waiting for sinners to bring their sacrificial
offerings to him. He is the agent throughout:

All is God's doing, as he rejoined us to himself through
Messiah, and made us cooperators in the rejoining. Just
as God was in Messiah rejoining creation to himself,
canceling man's sin, so he made us diplomats of the rejoining. (2 Cor 5.18–19)

Another Pauline letter says:

He is before all things, and all things cohere in him. He
is, in parallel, the head of the body that is the gathering.
He is the first-born out of death, making him in every
way primary. For it was God's glad will to invest in him
all the fullness of being, through him to rejoin all things
to himself, accomplishing peace through his blood from

the cross, peace for heaven and for earth through him.
(Col 1.17–20)

Jesus himself speaks of his mission as lifting humankind
up into his own intimacy with the Father:

"Just as you have shed your splendor on me, so I shed it
on them, so they may be at one with us, just as we are
one, I in them and you in me, so they may be fulfilled in
that oneness. So all creation may recognize that you
have sent me, and that you have loved them even as you
have loved me. Father, you have given them to me, and I
wish that they should be where I am, that they may see
the splendor you have given me out of the love you had
for me before laying the foundations of creation" (Jn
17.22–24).

Dark and mysterious as is the whole matter of the Incarnation and the Passion, perhaps a simple thing can help us
think of them. I turn to my own experience. My young son
woke up with a violent nightmare one night. When I asked
what was troubling him, he said that the nun in his school
had told the children they would end up in hell if they
sinned. He asked me, "Am I going to hell?" There is not an
ounce of heroism in my nature, but I instantly answered
what any father would: "All I can say is that if you're going
there, I'm going with you." If I felt that way about my son,

God obviously loves him even more than I do. Perhaps the Incarnation is just God's way of saying that, no matter what horrors we face or hells we descend to, he is coming with us. I did not realize at the moment that I was just following a way we should think of God, according to Jesus himself:

> "Would any one of you give your son a stone when he asked for bread, or a snake when he asked for fish? Well, if you, flawed as you are, know how to provide good things for your children, how much more will your Father in the heavens provide for those who ask it of him?" (Mt. 7.9–11)

Chesterton offers another way into the mystery, in a little two-act play of his called *The Surprise*. The play opens, in the Middle Ages, with a friar wandering through a woods. He sees a large rolling caravan, a platform stage with its curtain open and handsome life-size puppets lying with their strings loose. The puppet master is up above the stage. The friar asks what town he will be giving his show in—he would like to see it. The man tells him to sit down and he will give him a free performance. A romantic tale is then spun out in which a swashbuckling hero and his friend, drinking to each other's health, swear to rescue a damsel in captivity. They carry it off with great panache, and the play ends. The friar applauds, but the man asks to go to confession. He confesses that he is unhappy because he loves his characters, yet they do not breathe and reciprocate his love. As he turns away, the friar falls to his knees and prays that his wishes might come true. The curtain falls on the first act.

The second act begins with the puppets again lying down amid their loose strings. But then the characters begin to stir on their own. They rise and start reenacting the play. But this time little things begin to go wrong, each aggravating the next, and the pace of mishaps quickens. The friends drink too much and quarrel, they show jealousy over the heroine, they arrive too late to rescue her, so her captor is about to rape her. At this point, the puppet master stands up on the roof of the caravan and shouts, "Stop! I'm coming down." God is going with us. Now that his creatures have free will, the puppet master can no longer manipulate them from above. He must come down to be with them, to fight for them.

What I like about this parable is that there is no question about an "angry God." The maker is coming down to protect his creatures, from themselves and from all the consequences of their errors and sins. He is their champion, not their punisher. This shows that there are two ways of talking about what Paul called a rejoining. If we talk of salvation as sacrifice in the sense of appeasement or propitiation, there is a note of assuaging an angry God. If we talk of it as rescue, the power from which mankind has to be rescued is not God but the forces at work against God—all the accumulated sins that cripple human freedom. In the New Testament, this legacy of evil is personified as Satan. When Jesus, going to his death, says it is the enemy's time, and the dominion of darkness (Lk 22.53), he is certainly not saying that God is the dark power. Satan is. It is the struggle with the human capacity for evil that Jesus wages in the name of humanity. Human freedom and perversity have led the sheep astray, have condemned the prodigal son to his own degradation, and only the Shepherd and Father can send for his rescue. Similarly, when Jesus wept over the Jerusalem that was about to kill him as it killed the prophets (Mt 23.27), he was not suggesting that God killed the prophets. It was the enemy of God who did. It was Satan.

If we want to know why Jesus died, the best place to look for an explanation is in John's account of the Last Supper, in the long passage called the Last Discourse. This does not speak of divine anger to be allayed by sacrifice. It talks, over and over, of divine love entering into the human darkness and turning it to light:

> "I will no longer speak much with you, since the Prince of This World is upon us—though he has no power over me. But all creation must see that I love the Father, and I do whatever the Father has commanded me. Rise and let us be off from here." (Jn 14.30–31)

The Sacrifice

IF WE ASK WHY PAUL and others speak of our being rescued by Christ's blood, what does that mean if his blood is not a sacrifice to the Father? The Last Discourse tells us: "No one can show greater love than this, that he lay down his life for those he loves" (Jn 15.13). He sheds his blood with and for us, in our defense, not as a libation to an angry Father. That is how he sacrifices himself for us.

There are other references to Jesus' sacrifice in scripture. Paul talks of him as the *hilastērion*—which meant the golden covering on the Ark of the Covenant (Ex 25.17), known as the "mercy seat," where blood was sprinkled on the Day of Atonement: "In his blood God has presented him as the mercy seat for those who believe in him, to make clear his faithfulness to the covenant by canceling sin in his lenity" (Rom 3.25). Jesus is a new mercy seat, where his own blood, shed against man's enemy, becomes the bond with the Father. There is another famous passage where Paul speaks as if Jesus' blood were an expiation to the angry Father: "Though he [Jesus] was not conversant with sin, he [the Father] treated him as sin for our sake, so we might be God's vindication" (2 Cor 5.21). This continues a passage cited earlier where God initiates the rejoining with himself. Old commentators tried to make this mean that Jesus became a sinner, or even sin personified, or "a sin offering." But Jean-Noel Aletti shows rhetorically that it means Jesus was *treated as if* he were sin, in the sense that he is pitted against sin (Satan) and suffers the consequences by identification with sinful humanity. In the Epistle to the Hebrews, Jesus offers a sacrifice to God, but it is a unique kind of sacrifice, putting an end to all earlier kinds, and God initiates it to conquer sin, not to placate himself.

However we understand the mysterious sacrifice of the cross, one thing is certain—it is a proof of God's love, not his anger. "Such was God's love for the creation that he gave his only-begotten Son to keep anyone believing in him from perishing, to have a life eternal" (Jn 3.16). Jesus was sent to express, vindicate, and extend the Father's love. That is why the completion of his rescue raid into history is the descent into hell. This is not mentioned in the New Testament—save for a highly dubious reference in a notoriously obscure verse (1 Pet 3.19). But it is contained in the early creeds and baptismal oaths, showing that it is original to the revelation that was preached. For the Greek Orthodox Church, it is at the center of Jesus' mission—indeed, it is *the* Resurrection *(Anakatastasis)*. This is part of the whole conception of Jesus as the summation and climax of creation. He reaches back with his redeeming power to rescue mankind from the very beginning. Early poems and plays (especially in medieval treatments of it under the title of "the Harrowing of Hell"), along with endless paintings afterward, show Jesus breaking open the prison of the past to free those not previously vindicated in his blood. The normal depiction highlights the emergence, first, of Adam and Eve. Some pictures show him accompanied by the bandit who died with him. The comprehensiveness of God's salvific plan is emphasized—how

> Through black clouds the black sheep runs,
> And through black clouds the Shepherd follows him.

Though most depictions give the starring roles in this event to Adam and Eve, I believe the Shepherd was first seeking out his special lost one, Judas.

8. The Life of God

THE RESURRECTION OF JESUS is the proof, as the Song of Songs has it, that "Love is as strong as death" (Cant 8.6). The proof, as well, that Jesus was right to say, "I have the authority to lay down my life, and the authority to take it up again" (Jn 10.18).

Bishop N. T. Wright contends that only three interlocking things can give us confidence that Jesus is risen—the empty tomb, the multiple apparitions, and the seismic change in the followers of Jesus. The tomb's emptiness is a strong piece of evidence, since Jesus was buried in a conspicuous place, the new tomb where he would not taint other bodies by his unclean state. It would be easy to show that his body was still there, yet no early opponents of his followers could verify that.

Still, the empty tomb of itself means little or nothing. The body could have been moved, hidden, or neglected. It takes the apparitions both to draw attention to the empty tomb and to prove that it was not emptied by human design or accident. The apparitions in the gospels are multiple and confusing (if not contradictory)—the fruit of different communities' memory of their different founders and emissaries giving witness to what they saw. But the earliest and best testimony to the importance of the appearances—and to their astounding frequency—is Saint Paul's letters, written long before the gospels and well within the recent memory of his fellow Christians and their critics. He is the first and the steadiest reporter of Jesus' appearances to his followers (including himself):

> My main concern was to pass on to you what was passed on to me, that Christ died for our sins, in accord with the sacred writings, that he was buried, that he arose on the third day, in accord with the sacred writings, that he appeared to Kephas, then to the Twelve. After that, he appeared at the same time to more than five hundred of our brothers, many of whom are still with us, though some have died. And after that he appeared to James, then to all the emissaries. Last of all, he appeared to me, as by a late birth. (1 Cor 15.3–8)

Even these numerous appearances, spread out over places and times, would not indicate real resurrection without the empty tomb and the change in the followers. The appearances might have been ghostly or phantasmagorical, products of intense individual longing or mass hysteria. But the empty tomb finds its explanation and confirmation in the appearances, along with the psychic alteration in the first Christians. Because the empty tomb does not of itself mean that Jesus was risen, the interpretation of that emptiness is given in a customary biblical way by having angels proclaim the real meaning—a meaning reached by faith only after the appearances of Jesus to his followers.

These Christians were not expecting the Resurrection. They did not believe it, even when the women first announced it to them (Lk 24.11). They had, remember, all scattered and hidden as Jesus was condemned and executed. They were too timorous to go to the tomb, like the women, who also had no expectation that the body would not be there for them to anoint. Yet this band of cowards was suddenly changed into an energetic body of effective evangels, spreading their faith, firmly offering the claim that Jesus lives. Those unable to face the prospect of Jesus' death were soon embracing with great fortitude and hope their own martyrdom, at last knowing that what Jesus had told them was true: "As they persecuted me, they will persecute you" (Jn 15.20). Such solidity of faith did not have frail underpinnings. It was built on the firm interlocking evidence of the three things, the empty tomb, the multiple apparitions, and confidence in their own and their fellows' evidence.

It is true that Jesus appeared in numinous form, hard to interpret—his body was not the earthly body anymore, but one both outside time and space and affecting time and space. That is why he was not at first recognized by some (Mk 16.12, Lk 24.15–16, Jn 20.14, 21.4). The risen body is a mystery, though its evidence is tested and found true despite its numinous aspect. Paul, who saw the risen Jesus more than once (though *not* on the road to Damascus, where Luke says he only *heard* him), describes the difference between the first body and the risen one:

Will someone ask: In what way are the dead raised, and in what kind of body do they fare? Do not be a fool. Even a seed you sow does not come to life until it dies. And what you sow is not the plant it will become; it is a mere seed—of wheat, perhaps, or of some other grain. God gives it the plant he has assigned it, a different plant according what seed is sown. And all flesh is not the same, but that of humans, or of beasts or of bird or of fish. There are, moreover, heavenly bodies and earthly bodies, and the splendor of the heavenly bodies is one thing, the splendor of earthly bodies another. There is one splendor for the sun, another for the moon, and another for the stars—since star differs from star in splendor.

That is how it is with the resurrection of the dead. Sown disintegrated, the body is raised in integrity. Sown in disgrace, it is raised in splendor. Sown in frailty, it is raised in strength. What is sown as a sensate body is raised as a spiritual body. If there is a sensate body, there is also a spiritual body. For it is written, "The first man, Adam, became a living soul." But the last Adam became a life-giving spirit. Yet the spiritual comes not first; rather, the sensate is first, and then the spiritual. The first man came from the clay of earth, the second came from heaven. As the first man was of clay, so are the others clayey. And as the last man was from heaven, so are all his fellows heavenly. And as we have borne the likeness of the man of clay, so shall we bear the likeness of the man from heaven. (1 Cor 15.35–49)

To make it clear that the risen body of Jesus is now a spiritual body, yet one connected with its earthly "seed," Jesus allows himself to be touched by Thomas. Even more strikingly, he eats with those he appears to—with the wayfarers to Emmaus (Lk 24.30) and with the fishermen disciples on the shore (Jn 21.13). Why would he nurture a body that no longer needs sustenance? It is a mystical communing with his comrades in the basic image of the afterlife. People often wonder how they should imagine life after death. Jesus used the imagery of the scriptures, presenting it as a great welcoming banquet.

The Heavenly Banquet

"Happy the man who will feast in God's reign."
(Lk 14.15)

"I dispose my reign for you as my Father has disposed
it for me, that you may eat and drink at my table."
(Lk 22.29–30)

"I promise you that many will come from the East and
from the West to take their place at table with Abraham,
Isaac, and Jacob in heaven's reign." (Mt 8.11)

THE GREAT BANQUET is sometimes considered a wedding
feast, which unites all family and friends (Mt 22.1–14,
25.1–13, Rev 19.9). So Jesus' eating in his appearances after
the Resurrection is a proleptic and partial anticipation of the
feast that awaits us at what Chesterton called the Inn at the
End of the World. That was the meaning of the Last Supper,
too, where Jesus said, "In truth I tell you I shall from now on
drink no more the vine's offspring until the day I drink a
new wine in God's reign" (Mk 14.25). He is in God's reign
from the moment of his Resurrection.

We pray for the same proleptic eating of the future meal
in the Our Father: "The approaching bread give us even
today." The rare adjective for "approaching" is *epiousios*,

which can come from the words "to be" or from "to come." Those who derive it from "being" translate it as the bread-at-hand ("daily bread"). But the eschatological context of the whole prayer aligns this with the passage where Jesus says he has drunk only a little wine to anticipate the final banquet.

Many of his words and acts looked to the final banquet. The mark of this is the fullness and amplitude that presages a supreme fulfillment. This is always signaled by ecstatic *excess* in scripture—like the "water that gushed out in abundance" at a touch of Moses' wand, enough to satisfy everyone's thirst, or like the manna showered freely from heaven. So we read of a whole land flowing with milk and honey (Ex 3.8), or a river flowing with honey and curds (Job 20.17), or trees bearing fruit of every kind (Ez 47.12), or an overflowing cup (Ps 23.5).

When Jesus supplied feasts during his lifetime, he was not just satisfying a present hunger, but showing that he was bringing God's reign to fulfillment. At the marriage in Cana, he filled six huge vessels with wine of the most precious quality. Since each vessel held two to three measures, and a measure is about eight gallons, that makes sixteen to twenty-four gallons per vessel—96 to 144 gallons in all, far more than could be drunk by any party, no matter how large—and that was the point. He was indicating that he came to satisfy far deeper thirsts. As he told the Samaritan woman at the well where she drew water for him, "Anyone drinking from this well will be thirsty again; but anyone drinking from the water I shall give him will not thirst ever again. The water I shall give him will be an inner fountain of water bursting forth into eternal life" (Jn 4.14). In the same way, when he fed the four thousand or the five thousand, there was food *in excess*. With only five loaves and two fishes at the outset, he produced an eschatological overflow: "All of them ate all they wanted, yet the leftovers filled twelve huge hampers" (Mk 6.44). With four loaves to feed four thousand, he exceeded again: "They ate all they wanted, yet the leftovers were enough to fill seven hampers" (Mk 8.9).

Given all this rich imagery of the final banquet, given the foreshadowings of the Eucharist in the feedings of the four thousand and five thousand, it is clear that the Last Supper was the principal image of the afterlife, one confirmed when Jesus revealed himself to the couple at Emmaus in the breaking of the bread (Lk 24.30).

This was the meal that was to be repeated "to keep his memory until he comes" (1 Cor 11.25–26). The love meal (agape) was the home service by which the Christian gatherings expressed their unity in the mystical body of Christ.

Why, in the richness of this banquet tradition, would Benedict XVI, when he was Cardinal Ratzinger, say that it was unworthy to treat the Catholic Mass as a meal? Why would he say that altars should not allow the priest to face his brothers and sisters in Christ as across a dinner table? Why would he say that the priest should turn his back on the congregation and commune only with his God? Why would he say that others should not share in this activity of the priest, who is alone responsible for what occurs? Did he think that Jesus, at the Last Supper, stopped in the course of the meal, stood up, crossed a barrier separating him from his followers, and muttered to God in a language (Latin) neither he nor they understood?

The pope makes all these astonishing claims because he thinks the Mass is not a meal but a sacrifice, made by a priest. Not for him the Epistle to the Hebrews, which says that Christ is the unique priest making one last sacrifice. The pope, like his predecessors, is returning to the religion Jesus renounced, with all its paraphernalia of priesthood, separation from the laity, consecration of places and things, distance from the "unclean" life of those not privileged by consecration. This is what led to the idea that priests can say private Masses, without any community at all, since their consecrating words are all that is needed to repeat the sacrifice of Calvary, and the more such Masses are said the more the pleasing results of sacrifice are accumulated. In other words, we repeat what Jesus did at the Last Supper "to keep his memory" by doing what he never did there. I began this book by noting that we cannot be "other Christs," since he is God and we are not. But priesthood is an attempt to pretend that some men are other Christs, who can do what he did in his one sacrifice. Religion is still trying to kill Jesus.

We cannot be other Christs, we can only be members of Christ, in his risen and mystical body, in which there are no distinctions of the sort his first followers sought and Jesus refused to grant:

> Baptized into Messiah,
> you are clothed in Messiah,
> so that there is no more
> Jew or Greek,
> slave or free,
> man and woman,
> but all are one, are the same
> in Jesus Messiah. (Gal 3.26–28)

Augustine knew that the Jesus made present in the agape meal is present *in all his members,* not in the bread they share with each other. Commenting on John's gospel (6.50), he wrote, " 'This then is the bread that comes down from heaven, so that the one eating it shall not die.' But these words apply only to the validity of the mystery, not its visibility—to an inner eating, not an external one; to what the heart consumes, not what the teeth chew." And in Sermon 227, he reaffirms this: "The symbol is received, it is eaten, it disappears—but can Christ's body disappear, Christ's church disappear, Christ's members disappear?" In Sermon 272, he makes it clear that it is the *congregation* that becomes Christ in the agape meal:

> If you want to know what is the body of Christ, hear what the Apostle [Paul] tells believers: "You are Christ's body and his members" [1 Cor 12.27]. If, then, you are Christ's body and his members, it is your symbol that lies on the Lord's altar—what you receive is a symbol of yourselves. When you say "Amen" to what you are, your saying it affirms it. You hear "The body of Christ," and you answer "Amen," and you must *be* the body of Christ to make that "Amen" take effect. And why are you bread? Hear the Apostle again, speaking of this very symbol: "We, though many, are one bread, one body" [1 Cor 10.17].

Far from thinking that food at a meal is an unworthy way of speaking of the agape feast, Augustine explores deeper and deeper into the meaning of this mystery:

> The bread makes clear how you should love your union with one another. Could the bread have been made from one grain, or were many grains of wheat required? Yet

before they cohered as bread, each grain was isolated.
They were fused in water, after being ground together.
Unless wheat is pounded, and then moistened with water, it can hardly take on the new identity we call bread.
In the same way, you had to be ground by the ordeal of
fasting and exorcism in preparation for baptism's water,
and in this way you were watered in order to take on
the new identity of bread. But bread must be finished by
baking in fire. In this way you were being ground and
pounded, as it were, by the humiliation of fasting and
the mystery of exorcism. After that, the water of baptism moistened you into bread. But the dough does not
become bread until it is baked in a fire. And what does
fire represent for you? It is the anointing with oil [after
the water at baptism]. Oil, which feeds fire, is the mystery of the Holy Spirit. . . . The Holy Spirit comes
to you, fire after water, and *you are baked into the bread
which is Christ's body.* This is how your unity is
symbolized.

There are still some who see the meaning of the meals Christ
ate with his followers after his Resurrection. One of these
is the poet Denise Levertov, in her poem called "Ikon: The
Harrowing of Hell."

> Down through the tomb's inward arch
> He has shouldered out into Limbo

to gather them, the prophets,
the innocents just His own age and those
unnumbered others waiting here
unaware, in an endless void He is ending
now, stooping to tug at their hands,
to pull them from their sarcophagi,
dizzied, almost unwilling. Didmas,
neighbor in death, Golgotha dust
still streaked on the dried sweat of his body
no one had washed and anointed, is here,
for sequence is not known in Limbo;
the promise, given from cross to cross
at noon, arched beyond sunset and dawn.
All these He will swiftly lead
to the Paradise road: they are safe.
That done, there must take place that struggle
no human presumes to picture:
living, dying, descending to rescue the just
from shadow, were lesser travails
than this: to break
through earth and stone of the faithless world
back to the cold sepulcher, tearstained
stifling shroud; to break from *them*
back into breath and heartbeat, and walk
the world again, closed into days and weeks again,
wounds of His anguish open, and Spirit
streaming through every cell of flesh
so that if mortal sight could bear

> to perceive it, it would be seen
> his mortal flesh was lit from within, now,
> and aching for home. He must return
> first, in Divine patience, and know
> hunger again, and give
> to humble friends the joy
> of giving Him food—fish and a honey comb.

One of the many beauties of this poem is that it reminds us that Jesus still needs feeding. Our test for entry into heaven's reign is whether we fed Jesus in the hungry, clothed him in the naked, welcomed him in the outcast. It was the warmth of that sense of community that witnessed to Jesus' presence in the "primitive communism" of early Christianity.

Paul, writing in the fifties of the first century C.E., said that Jesus' appearance to him in the thirties was the last of the many post-Resurrection appearances to the followers (1 Cor 15.8). That is what is meant by Christ's Ascension, ending such appearances. Jesus has been with the Father from the moment of his Resurrection; but now he is no longer acting on history through his risen body. As usual, the theological meaning of this is put in the form of an angelic interpretation—the angel asks why the men of Galilee are still looking at the sky (Ac 1.10–11).

Jesus has not deserted his followers, but he acts now

through the Paraclete (Champion) he promised to send to his followers. That is the meaning of Pentecost, when the strengthened followers boldly go out to spread the good news of life in Christ. When the Spirit speaks though the followers, they are taken into the inmost communication of God with himself. The Trinity is the union-in-diversity that Chesterton spoke of when he said, "It is not good for God to be alone." The Spirit cries out to the Father through Christ, vivifying the mystical body of Christ in which his members act. Jesus was resurrected into us. We walk around living his life after his death. The Resurrection was not something that happened a long time ago, in a far place. It is happening now, everywhere on earth. He still slips into, through, and around the structures that would confine and confound him. He is still the "ragged figure flitting from tree to tree in the back of our minds."

Of course we followers misunderstand him at times, deny him like Peter, betray him like Judas. Of course the churches that call on his name return often to the forms of religion he renounced. But we know that he said, "Where two or three come together in my name, there am I, in their midst" (Mt 18.20). Such gatherings occur in all the Christian communities, and they form an invisible network, heeding the Lord's injunction against discriminating between his followers so long as they cast out the devils of division and discord in his name (Lk 9.49). The Spirit that touched the Lord's followers with fire at Pentecost leads them to cross all cultural barriers by speaking the universal language of love, which is the life of God. They live "knowing that he who raised Jesus, the Lord, will raise us along with him, and bring us to his side" (2 Cor 4.14).

Afterword

It is the simple contention of this book that what Jesus meant is clearly laid out in the gospels. He did not found a church or advocate a politics—though one can worship him in many gatherings or polities. But neither of those structures is what he meant by "the reign of heaven." Heaven's reign is himself, the avenue of access to the Father. He partly opened that access on earth, but the process will be complete only in the Father's bosom when history ends. One enters the heavenly reign by sharing Jesus' own intimacy with the Father. He is the Vine, to which the branches must be attached to draw life from him. By becoming members of his mystical body, one honors the Father and passes the key test for a disciple—treating the poor, the thirsty, the hungry, the naked as if they were Jesus.

How can we tell who among us is securely affixed to the Vine? We cannot. He told us as much. He says that heaven's reign on earth is like wheat growing with weeds in it, to be separated only at harvest time, when the wheat will be gathered into God's barn (Mt 13.24–30). Or it is like unsifted wheat with chaff in it, waiting for a final separation of the two (Mt 13.30). Or it is like a great net with "fish of all kinds" in it, the edible to be sorted out only after the catch is hauled in—another image of the final reign as a feast (Mt 13.47–48). The meaning is clear. All earthly societies have currently unidentifiable elements of heaven's reign in them, but none of them—no state, no church, no voluntary organization—can be equated with heaven's reign. Claims to a "faith-based politics" or to a perfect church substitute a false religion for heaven's reign—which is a form of idolatry.

Jesus' followers have the obligation that rests on all men and women to seek justice based on the dignity of every human being. That is the goal of politics, of "the things that belong to Caesar." But heaven's reign makes deeper and broader demands, the demands not only of justice but of love. Saint Augustine came in time to renounce the classical ideals of Plato and Aristotle, which exalted the intellect as man's noblest faculty. Augustine knew that the highest human faculty is love, the self-emptying love of Jesus: "A new instruction I have given you: Love one another. As I have loved you, you must also love one another. All will know that you are my followers by this sign alone, that you have love for one another" (Jn 13.34–35).

None knew better what Jesus meant than Saint Paul when he wrote:

Were I to speak the languages of all men and all angels, without having love, I were as a resonating gong or jangling cymbal. Were I to prophesy and know all secrets and every truth, were I to have faith strong enough to move mountains, without having love, I were as nothing. Were I to give away all my possessions, or give my body to be burned, without having love, it would avail me nothing.

Love is patient, is kind. It does not envy others or brag of itself. It is not swollen with self. It is not wayward or grasping. It does not flare with anger, nor harbor a grudge. It takes no joy in evil, but delights in truth. It keeps all confidences, all trust, all hope, all endurance. Love will never go out of existence. Prophecy will fail in time, languages too, and knowledge as well. For we know things only partially, or prophesy partially, and when the totality is known, the parts will vanish. It is like what I spoke as a child, knew as a child, thought as a child, argued as a child—which, now I am grown up, I put aside. In the same way we see things in a murky reflection now, but shall see them full face when what I have known in part I shall know fully, just as I am known. For the present, then, three things matter— believing, hoping, and loving. But supreme is loving. (1 Cor 13.1–13)

Acknowledgments

THIS BOOK was the idea of my editor, Carolyn Carlson—as was my previous book, *The Rosary*. I thank her, and my agent, Andrew Wylie.